**MIMESIS INTERNATIONAL**

PHILOSOPHY
n. 3

Daniela Tagliafico

PRETENSE A RELATIVIST ACCOUNT

MIMESIS
INTERNATIONAL

© 2014 – Mimesis International
www.mimesisinternational.com
e-mail: info@mimesisinternational.com
Book series: *Philosophy*, n. 3

Isbn: 9788857508023

© MIM Edizioni Srl
P.I. C.F. 0241937030

SUMMARY

ACKNOWLEDGEMENTS

I would like to thank, first of all, my tutor, Cristina Meini, who has always encouraged me during these years. My thanks also go to Margherita Arcangeli, Diego Marconi, Shaun Nichols, Giulia Piredda, Enrico Terrone and Alberto Voltolini, for their comments and suggestions on several aspects of this thesis.

I would also like to express my gratitude to Pierre Jacob, and to all members and students of the Institute Jean Nicod in Paris, for the amazingly good year that I spent there.

Finally, I would like to thank Maurizio Ferraris and my friends at the Laboratory for Ontology, who have become a second family to me.

PREFACE

Man is a make-believe animal:
he is never so truly himself as when he is acting a part.
William Hazlitt

The word "pretense" can be used in a twofold sense. When we say that somebody is pretending, we can mean either that somebody is playing around with us, make-believing that something is the case, or that the subject in question is trying to deceive us, making us believe something she does not really believe in. A child playing a game of make-believe, or an actor on the scene, playing a certain role, typically does not want to deceive her audience; on the contrary, she wants her make-believe to be recognized as such by her partners and spectators. A person who tells us a lie is instead deceiving us: by asserting something, she pretends to hold true what she is telling us, when, instead, this is not the case. So, while in a game of make-believe all participants in the game are aware of the pretense, in a case of deception only the make-believer is conscious of it.

In this book, we will be mainly concerned with the former kind of pretense – i.e. with make-believe – with the aim of explaining the architecture of the mind that is needed for such a capacity. This research will allow us to investigate more deeply the nature of certain mental states of ours and of some capacities that seem to be central to our social life. We will not take into consideration, however, the further and more sophisticated abilities that are required in order to conceal pretense: that is, how we can avoid other people from recognizing we are pretending.

The special interest that pretense deserves stems from the fact that, I think, even if there are some attestations of pretense behaviors in animals (for a review cf. Mitchell 2002), certainly these behaviors cannot be compared with human games of make-believe. In this sense, it seems that pretense can be counted among the marks of the human species alone, and that an exploration this activity is an exploration into what is most peculiar to human beings.

What is really puzzling with this ability is the fact that pretense seems to lack – at least at first sight – any usefulness. What could be, in fact, the advantage of acting according to an imaginary representation of the world, which does not correspond to the actual situation, instead of keeping a firm grip on reality? Why should children be encouraged to get involved in pretend scenarios, if they run the risk of getting confused?

The capacity for pretending, or better yet, the capacities for understanding pretense and participating in games of make-believe, seem to be quite sophisticated abilities, which children start to develop around the middle of their second year of life. In pretense, in fact, a subject must deal not only with her representations of some actual state of affairs, but also with her representations of an imaginary situation and, moreover, she must somehow project the latter on the former, acting accordingly. For example, an imaginary representation of a telephone can be projected onto the visual perception of a banana, in order for the subject to pretend to make a phone call; an empty cup can be imagined to be full of tea when we pretend to have a tea party; and a little girl can pretend to be *Belle*, living in an enchanted castle.

In the last fifty years, starting with the pioneering work done by Piaget (1945/1962), the literature on pretense has been continuously maturing, and nowadays it has reached immense proportions. Dozens of hypotheses have been formulated about the role played by pretense in our cognitive development. For example, Piaget insisted on the fact that pretend play would help the child to understand the arbitrariness of symbolic function, that is to say, the fact that anything can stand for anything

> J. mimes sleep while she is holding a cloth [...] instead of a pillow, [...] It can therefore no longer be said that the scheme [*of going to sleep*] has been evoked by its usual stimulus, and we are forced to recognize that these objects merely serve as substitutes for the pillow, substitutes which become symbolic through the actions simulating sleep. (Piaget 1945/1962: 97)

By using a piece of cloth as a pillow, little Jacqueline would come to appreciate the fact that something (a piece of cloth) can be a symbol for something else (a pillow). Other authors have pointed to the fact that pretense would make children more attentive to social signals, thus improving some important social skills, such as intention reading, social referencing, and joint attention (cf. e.g. Lillard 2001: 157-158). But pretense has been studied, in particular, in relation to another social ability, which is usually defined as "folk psychology" or "mindreading": that is, the capacity to understand and predict the behavior of other agents, as well as our own, on the basis of the attribution of mental states such as beliefs, desires, emotions, etc. For example, if I say that I am sure that my friend Giacomo will go to the cinema *Corallo* this evening because he *wants* to see the last movie about Che Guevara and he *believes* that this movie will be projected there, what I am doing is precisely an exercise in mindreading: I am predicting my friend's behavior by attributing to him certain mental states, which I suppose he entertains at the moment. Now, if we think to the abilities that are required by pretense, we can easily see why these two capacities are strictly related: when we pretend to do something, or to be someone, what we do is we imagine being in a different situation; and this act of imagination often requires that the pretender assumes not only another physical perspective, but also another mental perspective. That is, she has to imagine her own mental perspective in a different situation (what *she* would think and feel in that situation), or the mental perspective of another subject in a certain possible situation (what *someone else* would think and feel in that situation).

This is why we believe that any investigation of pretense needs to take into consideration, at least, the two related capacities of imagination and mindreading. As I will try to show, the conception of imagination one adopts is indispensable for developing a theory of pretense, in the sense that one cannot take a stance towards several questions concerning pretense – such as the so-called "cognitive quarantine" of our pretend representations, or the question of how pretend behaviors are motivated – if one does not preliminary choose between different conceptions of the imagination. Analogously, the way one conceives imagination is directly tied to the way one conceives the nature of mindreading, and thus to the way we are able to take someone's perspective and understand her mental states.

The special link that pretense entertains with imagination and mindreading also explains why the topic of pretense has received so much attention, not only in the domain of psychology, but also in those of philosophy of the mind and philosophy of the cognitive sciences. Understanding pretense means to reflect on the way we conceive our mental states: what their identity conditions are, what it means for a mind to re-instantiate certain kinds of mental states, which is the nature of imagination, how we represent mental states to ourselves, and so on.

The philosophical reflection on pretense, however, is extremely fragmentary. The only accounts of pretense which possess some exhaustiveness are that developed by Alan Leslie at the end of the '80s, the theory of representation elaborated by Joseph Perner (1991), and, more recently, the "cognitive theory of pretense" proposed by Shaun Nichols and Stephen

Stich (2000).[1] In the majority of cases what we find, instead, are quite extemporary reflections, often developed in the course of the discussion of related topics. Remarks on pretense and the cognitive abilities involved in this activity can be found, for example, in the aesthetic reflection about the nature of art and the nature of our emotional reactions towards fiction (cf. e.g. the theory developed by Kendall Walton in his 1990 book, *Mimesis as Make-Believe*) or in the discussion of the different theories of motivation. Also the theory proposed by Gregory Currie and Ian Ravenscroft (2002), concerning the recreative nature of our minds, is focused on the notion of imagination, whereas pretense is discussed only sporadically and often in an indirect manner.

The aim of this work has thus been twofold. On one hand, I have tried to make an effort to bring together different debates which, despite their apparent diversity, can be all related, for one reason or another, to the notion of pretense. On the other hand, I have aimed to offer a new account of pretense, which relies on the relativist conception of the mind developed by François Recanati (2007). The book is articulated in 6 chapters.

In the first, I have introduced the three main notions which I have dealt with in the rest of the book, namely: pretense, imagination, and mindreading. The aim was to give a first sketch of the major issues concerning each notion, and in particular to figure out the different ways in which they are intertwined.

Chapter 2 is devoted to the analysis and comparison of two different theories of the imagination, and to the evaluation of the consequences that they have for a theory of pretense. In particular, I have taken into consideration and contrasted the theory developed by Nichols and Stich (2000) with the "recreativist theory" of the imagination, formulated by Currie and Ravenscroft (2002) and proposed, more recently, also by Goldman (2006a, b). As I have tried to show, these theories can be seen as two opposite solutions to one and the same problem, that of defining the special status of an imaginative state, and both are, for different reasons, quite problematic.

In chapter 3 I have taken into consideration the problem of motivation in pretense. In particular, I have opposed, again, the theory proposed by Nichols and Stich – according to whom our behavior in pretense would

---

1   One could wonder why I consider Leslie's and Perner's theories as philosophical accounts of pretense, since they are both psychologists and their theories are grounded on empirical work. However, they also contain some important reflections on the nature of mental representations in general and on the alteration that pretense provokes on the standard semantic relations holding between the mind and the world.

be motivated by a genuine desire to act in accordance with the imagined scenario – to the recreativist account endorsed by Currie and Ravenscroft (2002) and Goldman (2006a, b) – according to whom, instead, pretense requires not only belief-like imaginings, but also desire-like imaginings, that is, imaginings which play the same functional role as desires – questioning, in particular, the idea itself that we can speak of "pretend desires".

Chapter 4 discusses the question of the metarepresentational abilities which are required by pretense. I have started with the famous theory of pretense proposed by Leslie (1987, 1994), as well as the different notions of metarepresentation that have been attributed to him. I have then reviewed the most important criticisms that have been moved against Leslie's theory and evaluated some alternative accounts, according to which it would be possible to understand and engage in pretense without making use of any metarepresentational ability (cf. e.g. Perner 1991; Olson 1993; Suddendorf & Whiten 2001) or by appealing to a minimal form of metarepresentation (Meini & Voltolini 2010).

In chapter 5 I have laid the foundations for my own account of pretense. More precisely, I have taken into consideration the relativist account of our mental states that Recanati proposed in his *Perspectival Thought* (2007), trying to define in detail how imagination can be conceived within this framework.

Finally, in chapter 6 I have developed my own account of pretense. I have thus tried to specify the architecture of the mind that derives from embracing a Strong Moderate Relativist framework such as the one proposed by Recanati, and consequently, the peculiar nature of a pretend mental state within this architecture. In particular, I have tried to outline the kinds of advantages offered by this relativist account, which allows us to explain some peculiar features of pretense such as the *anchoring* of our imaginings to our perceptions and the capacity to keep our pretend representations *quarantined* from our genuine mental states.

I.
PRETENSE, IMAGINATION AND MINDREADING

The capacity for pretending is often discussed in relation to two other capacities: imagination and metarepresentation. Pretending to be someone or to do something seems to imply, in fact, the capacity to imagine a certain possible situation; and this, in turn, requires either the assumption of a merely physical perspective or, rather, of a different mental perspective. For example, if I decide to pretend being in a jungle, I can simply imagine walking in a forest, cutting down the undergrowth, sweating, or listening to some exotic bird hidden in the brush. In addition to this, however, I can also take the mental perspective of that 'me' in that possible situation: I can thus imagine feeling tired and dehydrated, being afraid because I got lost, hoping that someone is looking for me, and so on. The same holds true if I pretend to be someone else, for example, if I pretend to be Napoleon, waiting for Waterloo's battle. In this case, I can try to imagine how the battlefield could have appeared to Napoleon, how the disposition of the soldiers was but, at the same time, I can also imagine his feelings, his excitement for the imminent fight, his worries, etc. In this sense, then, pretense implies the possession of a specific kind of imaginative ability: that is, mindreading, the capacity to understand the mental states that one would possess in a certain imaginary situation.

Pretense, however, seems to require something more than this. In order to entertain both the physical and mental perspective of another subject (or one's own perspective) in a certain possible situation, in fact, one must be able to keep her imaginative states distinct from her genuine beliefs and desires, that is: one must be able to keep the pretend representation "that is a cake" separate from her genuine belief "That is a muddy object"[1]. This seems to require some form of metarepresentation, which means the

---

1   From now on, we will use the expressions "pretend representation" or "pretend mental state" – as opposed to a real or "genuine mental state" – to refer to those representations that are supposed to guide our behavior during an episode of pretense. Pretend representations are thus as real as genuine representations, but they

capacity to represent the mental states themselves as such, i.e. as mental representations of some sort (imaginings *vs.* beliefs or desires, etc.).

In this chapter we will start with a first characterization of the relationship between pretense, imagination and mindreading, whereas we will approach the question of the role played by metarepresentation only in the fourth chapter. Let us begin with the discussion of some issues about pretense and, more precisely: the opposition between two different definitions of pretense (§ 1.1), its possible contents (§ 1.2), its defining properties (§ 1.3) and, finally, the different forms of pretense that have been individuated (§ 1.4). Then, we will more closely investigate the relationship between pretense and imagination, and in particular, the question whether or not imagination is necessary for pretending (§ 2.1); the different ways in which imagination can be involved in pretense (§ 2.2); the difference between creative and recreative imagination as well as the important debate concerning the unity of the imagination (§ 2.3). Finally, we will take into consideration the relationships between pretense and mindreading. We will thus recall the fundamental distinction between two different conceptions of the nature of mindreading, namely, the theory-theory and the simulation theory of mindreading (§ 3.1), paying special attention to the distinction between "moderate" (§ 3.2) and "radical" simulation (§ 3.3), and conclude with some final remarks concerning the relationship between imagination and simulation (§ 3.4).

1. *Pretense*

1.1. *Behavioral* vs. *mentalistic conceptions of pretense*

A first problem about pretense concerns its definition. Pretense is often described – at least at a first attempt – as *behaving as-if*: the pretending subject is a subject who behaves as if something – a certain state of affairs *p* – were the case. For example, the child who pretends that a banana is a telephone, acts upon the banana (she holds the banana next to her ear, she talks into the banana, etc.) as if she acted upon a telephone; the girl who pretends to be a princess, speaks and acts as if she were a princess, and so on.

This definition, however, does not seem to be sufficient in order to characterize pretense and distinguish it from other cases, such as *acting in error*

---

differ from genuine representations for the role they play within the cognitive architecture of the mind.

or a *functional play.* As remarked by Alan Leslie (1987: 413), the child acting upon a banana as if it were a telephone, could simply be wrong and truly believe that the banana she is holding in her hands is not a fruit, but rather a telephone. A person behaving as Napoleon could be a deluded subject, really believing to be the French emperor. Alternatively, as stressed by Huttenlocher and Higgins (1978), the child we suppose to be pretending could be simply showing a symbolic activity. For example, while setting out a tea scenario – e.g. setting the table, filling the cups with some liquid, etc. – the child could be merely aiming to demonstrate her knowledge of the conventional use of objects; in this case the toy cups, which are only a pretend replica to us, could be seen by the child as ordinary objects with conventional uses (cf. Leslie 1987: 413).

Other authors have also recognized this point. Angeline Lillard, for example, observes (2001: 497):

> if a child (the pretender) is pretending a box (the reality) is a boat, the child must be mentally representing a boat. To simply row the box around without representing it as a boat is not 'pretending the box is a boat'; it is simply acting like the box is a boat. One might do this if one were mistaken about boxes and their actual role in the world; one might also do this if one were demonstrating rowing. But such acts would not be boat pretenses unless a certain mental stance was taken.

In order to distinguish these cases from cases of true pretense, Leslie has thus claimed, a *behavioral account* of pretense is insufficient; what we need is rather a *mentalistic account.* Understanding that someone is pretending, in other words, requires the attribution to the pretender of a peculiar kind of mental state, pretense, which relates the agent with both an aspect of the actual situation and a possible state of affairs (Leslie 1987: 417; 1994: 217).

As we will see in greater detail in chapter 4, however, Leslie's argument has been contrasted by other accounts (Harris & Kavanaugh 1993; Lillard 1993, 2001; Nichols & Stich 2000), according to which pretending would not require the mastering of the concept of 'pretense' itself (and thus of this quite complicated state of mind), but only some more primitive capacity to understand that pretend actions do not correspond to the way the world is, but to some representation of a possible state of affairs, and thus to keep our genuine representations separate from our pretend ones.

To sum up, although the majority of researchers agree that a behavioral definition of pretense falls short of giving a satisfying definition of this capacity, no general agreement exists about what should be ascribed to the pretending subject in addition, of course, to the appropriate behavior. We will come back to this issue in chapter 4, as we will discuss which kinds of metarepresentational abilities pretense requires.

1.2. *Counterfactual and actual scenarios*

Another important issue about pretense concerns the contents of our pretend representations. Pretense is usually described as an activity that necessarily involves the depiction of a counterfactual scenario. For example, the table is dry, and we imagine that it is wet; in my hand I have a banana, but I imagine that it is a telephone; the seat in front of me is empty, but I imagine that a friend of mine is there, and so on. In other words, if p holds true in the actual situation, pretending seems to imply that, while we believe that p, we imagine a counterfactual situation where $\neg p$ is the case. As it has been shown by Nichols (2006a), however, this is not always the case.

In his 1994 paper, Leslie describes an experiment in which an adult (the experimenter) and a child play together according to a typical tea-party scenario. In front of the child there are two empty cups. The experimenter encourages the child to fill up both cups with some pretend juice or tea; then, he picks up one of the cups, turns it upside down, shakes it, and replaces it next to the other cup. At this point, the child is asked to point first to the full cup and then to the empty cup, although, of course, both cups are empty and have kept empty during the whole experiment.

Commenting on this experiment, Nichols (2006a: 6-7) remarks that, at the end of the pretense episode, we can attribute two different mental states to the child, a belief and an imagining, with exactly the same content p ("That cup is empty"). On the one hand, in fact, the child certainly believes that both cups are empty. This belief comes directly from her visual perception: the child sees the cups, she sees that no real liquid has been poured into them, and thus plausibly possesses, for each cup, a belief with the content "that cup is empty". On the other hand, however, when asked to point to the empty cup, the child does not point randomly, but chooses the cup that has been filled and then poured during the pretense episode. This shows that the child imagines of one cup – the cup that has been (pretendedly) poured – that it is empty.

This example, Nichols thus claims, is a proof of the fact that the same content p, "that cup is empty", can be entertained both as the content of what is usually called "a perceptual belief" and as the content of a state of imagination: not only the child believes that p, but she also imagines the very same proposition. Nichols thus concludes that when we pretend that *p*, we do not have to imagine something necessarily false: the contents of our imaginative states can well be states of affairs that also subsist in the actual world.

1.3. Defining properties

Different accounts of pretense have proposed different groups of features as the defining properties of pretense. In this paragraph, we will try to give a list of these properties. Without any pretension of exhaustiveness, our aim will be simply to present the most important issues that every account of pretense is called to address.

In their "cognitive account of pretense," Shaun Nichols and Steven Stich (2000) have individuated five characteristic features of pretense: (1) an initial premise; (2) an inferential elaboration; (3) a non-inferential elaboration; (4) the production of an appropriate behavior; and finally, (5) the cognitive quarantine of pretend states. These features, according to the authors, are to be considered as necessary properties of pretense, and thus, they claim, any account of pretense should be able to accommodate them all. Let us consider them in more detail.

(1) *The initial premise*. According to Nichols and Stich, pretense typically starts with an initial premise or a set of premises: for example, in the already-mentioned scenario ideated by Leslie (1994), the child and the experimenter both share the assumption that they are going to have a tea party. Moreover, the premises can either be spontaneously generated by the subject or by some other participant into the game. In the latter case, the subject has to figure out what the premise could consist of – if it has not been made explicit – and then she can decide whether or not she wants to engage in pretense. For example, in the banana-as-a-telephone scenario (Leslie 1987), the child has to infer, from the mother's behavior – mother holding the banana next to her ear and speaking into it – that her pretended goal is to make a telephone call. Once the premise has been correctly understood, the child typically begins to participate in the game, thus producing a behavior appropriate to the pretend scenario (e.g. asking the mother to have the receiver and talking into it).

(2) *Inferential elaboration*. The inference mechanisms are required not only to figure out the initial premise, but also to fill out the details of the game of make-believe. To come back to the tea-party scenario, when the experimenter pretends to fill an empty cup with some tea, and then turns the cup upside down, the child spontaneously concludes that the cup has been poured and that the table now is wet. In order to come to this conclu-

sion, Nichols and Stich say (2000: 119), the child has to rely on different sources of information: her current perceptions (what the pretender is doing with the cup), her memory of what has just happened in the game (the cup has been just filled with some tea), her background knowledge (what happens if a cup is turned upside down), and perhaps other sources as well. On the basis of this information, she will easily draw an inference and conclude that the cup has been poured.

(3) *Non-inferential elaboration.* Pretend situations are also elaborated in a non-inferential way. Nichols and Stich (2000: *ibidem*) appeal to two different examples, both concerning a restaurant scenario. In the first case, the person pretending to be the waiter gives the diner a menu, which consists only of a blank sheet of paper: the diner looks at the menu, pretends to read from it, and then announces that he will have chicken pasta. In this case, Nichols and Stich remark, the diner has no cues to infer what he should choose, so he has to appeal to his fantasy in order to 'fill the gaps' in the story and go on with the pretense.

This appeal to fantasy also occurs in the second example, although in this case the imagined event importantly departs from reality. In this case, after the diner's request for a sharper knife, the waiter pretends to carry a Japanese sword, instead of the usual meat knife, and then he also pretends to involuntarily cut off the diner's head.[2] As confirmed by a post-pretense interview, while in the former case the pretender judged his pretense as coherent with the choices he would have made in an analogous real situation, in the latter situation the waiter admitted to have chosen to act in a way he would never have acted in reality (2000: *ibidem*).

This shows that the non-inferential elaboration of a pretend scenario can either be produced in accordance to our knowledge of what would or should typically happen in an analogous real situation, or by 'breaking the rules,' that is by imagining a situation that could or should never happen for real. We will come back to this point at (6).

(4) *Appropriate behavior.* In addition to inferential and non-inferential elaboration, pretense also requires the adoption of an appropriate behavior, that is a behavior suitable to the imagined scenario. With respect to this feature, however, two questions arise: (1) on the one hand, one could ask how the pretenders know that they should behave in a certain manner – e.g. that "they should walk around making jerky movements and saying 'Chugga

---

2   The transcription of the whole conversation can be found in the online version of this paper, available at http://www.hum.utah.edu/philosophy/faculty/nichols/Onlinepapers.htm, and also in Nichols & Stich 2003: 22-24.

chugga, choo choo' when pretending to be a train." (2000: 120); (2) on the other hand, one could wonder why they do so, that is, what *motivations* they have to participate in pretense.

We will come back to these questions later, while discussing the ways in which imagination can guide our actions (cf. ch. 3). It is worth noting, however, that by saying pretense requires an appropriate behavior, one does not necessarily mean that pretense requires *action*. Although action characterizes the vast majority of games of make-believe, action is involved neither continuously nor necessarily. For example, in pretending to be a dead cat, I could simply lay down completely motionless, my eyes closed, but this would not mean that I am not pretending: my behavior – that is, my laying down without moving or talking – counts as the appropriate behavior for the content of this pretense. In this sense, then, action and custom are not necessary, but are only optional features of pretense.

(5) *Cognitive quarantine.* Finally, Nichols and Stich remark, pretense episodes seem to have effects only within pretense. The tea-party scenario, once again, provides a clear example: when the child observes the experimenter filling up the cup with some (imagined) liquid and then turning the cup upside down, she easily comes to the conclusion that the tea has been poured on the table, but she does not expect the table to be really wet, neither does she tries to dry it. In other words, her imaginative states are kept separate from her beliefs about the real world, and seem to have no influence on her behavior outside the game of make-believe.

Some authors, however, have also pointed to the existence of systematic exceptions to quarantine. Tamar Szabó Gendler (2003: 125; 2006), for example, speaks of the phenomenon that she calls *contagion*, which can concern, on her view, the sphere of our emotions as well as that of other 'cold' states.

Affective contagion is certainly the most frequent case and has long been discussed in aesthetics.[3] A typical example, Szabó Gendler says (2003: *ibidem*), is that of a child who, after having imagined that a bear is on the staircase, is reluctant to go upstairs alone. Although she knows that the bear is only a product of her imagination, she cannot avoid being afraid.[4]

---

3   The phenomenon of affective contagion has given rise, in aesthetics, to what has been called "the paradox of fiction" or the "paradox of fictional emotions", to distinguish it from other paradoxes concerning fiction (cf. e.g. Walton 1978, 1990, 1997; Currie 1990, 1997; Levinson 1990; Szabó Gendler & Kovakovich 2005). We will come back to this issue in chapter 3.

4   One could object that, in the case of children, it could be that the child really believes that there is a bear on the staircase, so her emotional reaction would be the

But cases of affective contagion, Szabó Gendler observes, are also our emotional reactions to fiction. In all of these cases, although the subject is perfectly aware of the fact that what she is attending is not real, she cannot avoid having some emotional reaction towards it. Charles – to cite a well-known example by Kendall Walton (1978: 5) – who is watching a horror movie about a terrible green slime "emits a shriek and clutches desperately at his chair", although, of course, he perfectly knows that the slime cannot endanger him. In this case, as well as in the child's case, it seems that the subject is not able to keep her imaginings completely quarantined, so that they cannot affect her behavior outside the pretend context.

In addition to the five features figured out by Nichols and Stich, four other important aspects of pretense should be mentioned.

(6) *Mirroring & disparity.* As seen above in the restaurant scenarios (cf. point 3), when we are involved in a game of make-believe, we can decide either to act in accordance to what would happen in an analogous real situation, or to depart from reality and suppose that in the pretense world things would happen in a way they would not, or could not happen in the real world (as seen, as the waiter brings the diner a Japanese sword instead of a meat knife). While discussing the distinctive features of pretense, Szabó Gendler (2003) takes into consideration precisely these two phenomena, which she labels, respectively, as *mirroring* and *disparity*.

Mirroring, Szabó Gendler says, is the phenomenon according to which "features of the imaginary situation that have not been explicitly stipulated are deriv[ed] via features of their real-world analogues", or, more simply, it is the case in which the "imaginative content is taken to be governed by the same sorts of restrictions that govern believed content" (2003: 125). Exactly as quarantine, which admits contagion, also mirroring is characterized by some systematic exceptions, that is, by cases in which the content of the imagination dramatically differs from the contents of our genuine beliefs: these cases are what Szabó Gendler calls "disparity".

More precisely, disparity can take two forms. On the one hand, the content of imagination can be *incomplete*: "there may be no fact of the matter (in the pretense) just how much tea has spilled on the table" (2003: *ibidem*). On the other hand, it can be *incoherent*: in pretense, Szabó Gendler says (2003: 126), a refrigerator can also have the function of a mathematical-

---

consequence of entertaining a real belief. However, the phenomenon of affective contagion has also been found in cases where the children were perfectly aware that a certain situation (e.g. the presence of a monster in a box) was pretend (cf. Szabó Gendler 2003: 132).

truth inverter. In other words, entities in pretense can bear, at the same time, incompatible properties. In this sense, then, Szabó Gendler traces a distinction between those contents that imagination can share with belief, and those that seem to be peculiar to imagination alone.

(7) *Yoking*. From the developmental point of view, Leslie observes, pretense shows a quite extraordinarily feature: the emergence of the capacity for solitary pretending always comes along with the capacity for pretending with other people and for recognizing pretense in others. In other words, not only do children by the age of 2 show the ability to engage in different kinds of pretense, but they are equally able to recognize whether another person is pretending or not, and engage in collective forms of pretense. These latter are two capacities that should be more demanding from a cognitive point of view, because the child is supposed to understand the intentions of other pretenders and adapt her behavior to them. Since there are no *a priori* reasons to think that these capacities should be yoked and emerge together, Leslie claims (1994: 215), a cognitive theory of pretense must be able to explain also this strange – and presumably not accidental – phenomenon[5].

(8) *Anchoring*. Another feature which Leslie points at is the phenomenon he calls "anchoring", i.e. the fact that in pretense the imagined content is always related to some particular aspect of the *here-and-now* situation (1994: 216). "For example," Leslie says, "it is *this* banana that mother pretends is a telephone, not bananas in general nor *that* banana over there. The pretended truth of the content, 'it is a telephone,' is thus anchored in a particular individual object in the here and now". In this sense, pretense not only implies that the subject is contemporarily aware of two different representations (one of the actual situation, the other of a possible one), but she must have established a link between them. The same feature has been highlighted by Lillard (2001: 497), who speaks of the necessity to *project* the mental representation that guides pretense into reality. Lillard also stresses the fact that it is precisely this feature that distinguishes pretense from mere imagination: "If one is simply imagining a boat, projection is not necessarily occurring. In pretense one imaginatively projects a particular boat onto a particular box".

(9) *Intentionality*. Finally, commenting on the phenomenon of projection – or anchoring, to use Leslie's terminology – Lillard (2001) has also stressed the fact that this projection must always be intentional. Relying on an observation made by Searle (1975: 325), according to whom "one cannot truly be said to have pretended to do something unless one intended to

---

5   We will analyze in detail the solution proposed by Leslie in chapter 4.

pretend to do it", Lillard has emphasized the fact that this projection must always be an intentional act. Without this requirement, Lillard says, also cases of psychopathological projection (as when a psychotherapist patient projects his mother onto the therapist) could count as instances of pretense. This, however, is not the case precisely because, whether or not the patient is aware of what she is doing, her projection is certainly not intentional, and thus we cannot count it as a case of pretense (2001: 498).

1.4. *How many kinds of pretense are there?*

Another question that could be posed about pretense is whether we should speak of it by using the singular or the plural form: that is, when we discuss pretense, are we dealing with a singular phenomenon, or with different phenomena, characterized by quite distinct features?

Leslie (1987: 414; 1994: 215) has argued for the existence of three fundamental kinds of pretense, each corresponding to the suspension of one of three different kinds of semantic relation (the relation possibly holding between a representation and its content).

(1) In *object substitution pretense* the semantic relation concerned is *reference*. Pretending that a banana is a telephone is a typical example of this form of pretense: as we have seen, in this game of make-believe one pretends a real object (a banana) is some other object (a telephone) and this implies, Leslie says, "a decoupling of the internal representation for telephones from its normal *reference* so that it functions in context as if it referred to a member of some arbitrary class of object" (1994: 215).

(2) In *properties pretense*, on the contrary, a given object or situation – for example a dry table – is pretended to have some property it does not really have – e.g. it is pretended to be wet. In this case, Leslie says, "the pretense decouples the normal effects of *predicating* wetness in the internal representation" and thus concerns the semantic relation of *truth* (1994: *ibidem*).

(3) Finally, *imaginary objects pretense* implies the suspension of the *existence presuppositions* that characterize a representation. This happens, for example, when we pretend that our teddy bear has a hat on his head. In this case an imaginary object is pretended to exist and thus we pretend that our internal representation really has content, when in fact it does not.

A cognitive theory of pretense, Leslie argues, must explain why there are three and exactly these three forms of pretense.[6]

---

6   Also Nichols and Stich (cf. 2000: 140) have accepted the existence of these three
      forms of pretense.

A different – although partly overlapping – distinction has been traced by the philosopher Amie Thomasson (2003) in the context of a wider proposal concerning the construction of social reality. What Thomasson proposes is to substitute the famous Searlian rule for the construction of social reality, "x [the physical object] counts as y [the social object] in context C" (Searle 1995), with some more detailed rules, that can be directly derived from those rules that set up our games of make-believe. In this sense, then, according to Thomasson, the construction of social reality would mirror exactly that of pretense reality.

All games of make-believe, Thomasson says, rise from the collective acceptance of one of the three following rules. The first, labeled "Singular Rule," takes the form:

"Of *a*, we collectively accept F*a*" [7],[8]

where *a* denotes a certain object in the real world and F a feature that we imagine the object possesses (2003: 280). In this kind of game, all participants accept that a certain real object or individual *a* – for example, a child – possesses a certain imaginary property F – for example, the property of being a princess. Pretense thus concerns a specific individual, but it can be extended, Thomasson remarks after Walton (1990), to all individuals that share a certain property. In this case we obtain a "Universal Rule" of the kind (2003: 281):

"For all *x*, we collectively accept that, if *x* meets all conditions in context C, then F*x*."

---

7   One could ask whether these rules should be considered as the initial premises of different kinds of pretend play (cf. § 1.3). This is not necessarily the case. They are constitutive rules, which can intervene at every moment in a game of make-believe and can be 'combined' with other rules which hold true in the same game. For example, a child could start his game of make-believe by deciding that he is a knight, walking in a forest. So, "of *a* (himself), he accepts F*a* (that he is a knight)". After playing for a while, the child could decide that every stump he will encounter, from that moment on, will count as a bear. So, "of *x* (the object encountered), he accepts that, if *x* meets all conditions in context C (if *x* is a stump in the real world), then F*x* (that object will have the property of being a bear)". In this case, then, the child does not start a new pretense, but enriches the present context of pretense with a new assumption.

8   Thomasson also specifies after Walton (1990) that, although these rules "must be at least implicitly understood and accepted in order to do their work, they may or may not be explicitly stipulated. They may simply be embodied in background knowledge and practices – as we, say, become competent players of children's games, appreciators of art, or members of society – and need not be something the participants explicitly have in mind or can verbally articulate" (2003: 279).

According to this rule, "if *anything* meets certain conditions, then it counts as having a particular [...] feature" (2003: *ibidem*). For example, in a game of make-believe, we can decide that every stump we encounter counts as a bear, i.e. for every object that satisfies the identity conditions for a stump, we imagine that it is a bear.

Contrary to Leslie, then, Thomasson does not seem to take into account the distinction between *object substitution* and *properties pretense* traced by the former: although she gives examples of both kinds of pretense – the child who pretends to be a princess is a typical instance of properties pretense, whereas the stumps which count as bears obviously are a case of object substitution pretense – she does not assign any particular relevance to the difference between the two cases. Rather, she points at another distinction, that between a pretense which concerns a singular object, which the attention is focused on, and a pretense which concerns every object belonging to a certain class, those objects are also included which are still unknown to the pretenders and waiting to be discovered (as in the case of the stumps hidden in the woods).

Finally, the third type of make-believe game (typical of fictional works) relies on an "Existential Rule," according to which:

> "We collectively accept that, if all conditions C obtain, then there is some x such that Fx."

For example, in the context of pretense, I can imagine that there is a hat on my teddy bear, or that there is a cup on the table, when, instead, nothing corresponds to this description. This kind of rule differs from the previous two since it does not introduce new facts about a certain aspect of reality, but rather, it introduces a new 'piece' of reality (2003: 282). In this sense, Thomasson remarks, this rule does not require an imagining *de re* – that is, it does not require that we imagine a certain real-world aspect, which has a fictional property F, as it was in the previous two cases – but it requires that we imagine *de dicto* that something exists.

Thomasson thus points to another semantic distinction, different from the ones identified by Leslie and, accordingly, she individuates two basic kinds of pretense: whereas in some cases (the cases described by the first two rules) the subject is related to a certain specific object, or a certain specific class of objects, in other cases (corresponding to the third rule) the subject is related only to a proposition.

Other forms of pretense, as we will see in the next section (cf. § 2.2), have been distinguished, instead, depending on the different involvement that imagination can have in pretense. More precisely this is about different forms of pretense, which can be individuated depending on the motivational role played by imagination in our games of make-believe.

2. *Imagination*

Speaking generally, in pretense, imagination seems to be required in order to produce a mental representation of some possible state of affairs – a representation that is somehow 'anchored at' or 'projected on' some aspect of the actual world and that typically guides the pretender's behavior. But is imagination a necessary ingredient of pretense, or can we figure out some forms of pretense that do not involve imagination? And how, exactly, should we describe the relationship between these two notions? Can imagination be a motivating aspect of pretense? Moreover, is there a unity of the imagination – i.e. can we speak of imagination as a single phenomenon – or should we distinguish, under this label, quite different mental activities? And, in the latter case, are all of them involved in pretense?

These are the questions we will deal with in this section.

2.1. *Is imagination a necessary ingredient of pretense?*

According to the analysis we have conducted in the previous section, imagination would seem to be a necessary ingredient of pretense. Pretending, we have said, always implies the depiction of a non-actual scenario: be it a counterfactual scenario or even, as shown by Nichols (cf. § 1.2), a scenario that is perfectly identical, in its content, to the actual situation. Some authors, however, have rejected this claim and argued that, exactly as imagining can occur without pretending, we can also have cases of pretense that do not require any involvement of the imagination. For example, Alan White (1990: 150ff.) has suggested the case of an impostor who pretends to be an aristocrat. There is no need, he has claimed, that her pretense be accompanied by an act of imagination. The impostor could simply adapt her appearance and behavior to how aristocrats typically look and act, without imagining that she is one, or visualizing herself as one.[9] Consequently, he has argued that imagining and pretending are different and independent capacities.

---

9   Although the example offered by White is a case of deception, rather than one of make-believe, his thesis seems to hold for every kind of pretense.

Though one could agree with this claim and recognize that, in principle, one could pretend without imagining, I think it is important to recognize that it is hardly possible to figure out an entire episode of pretense that happens without any appeal to the imagination. In particular, even if White is right in claiming that the impostor could pretend to be an aristocrat without *imagining herself* as an aristocrat, this is not the same as claiming that she could pretend to be an aristocrat – at least for more than some seconds – without any recourse to the imagination. While pretending, in fact, the impostor needs to imagine, at least, how her pretense will develop in the following moments, that is, how she wants the fiction to go on, and thus she needs to figure out the future contents of her pretense. Moreover, she will have to imagine which mental states the people she is talking to at a certain moment entertain and how to manipulate them, etc.

In conclusion, it is very difficult to figure out a pretend scenario which completely excludes the intervention of the imagination. To the extent to which a subject is conforming her behavior to some possible (non-actual) state of affairs, it seems that imagination is involved, if not necessarily, at least in every episode that lasts for more than a few moments.

2.2. *Four scenarios*

In their book *Recreative minds* (2002: 119-124), Gregory Currie and Ian Ravenscroft have figured out four different scenarios, each depicting a different relationship between pretense and imagination, or better, a different role played by imagination during an episode of pretense. The authors consider the case of Walter, a man who is playing a typical war game, endowed with toy guns, paint pellets, and the like. Walter's goal is to shoot the other players with these special pellets, while trying to avoid being shot: he is thus engaged in a series of behaviors like hiding behind a tree, jumping out at someone, shooting pellets, and so on. This behavioristic description of Walter's moves, however, admits at least four different psychological descriptions.

(1) The first, Currie and Ravescroft say, does not involve pretending at all. This is the case in which Walter treats the game precisely as a game, and not as a pretend scenario. For example, he thinks of his action of hitting with paint pellets as "hitting with paint pellets" and not as "shooting to kill," and thinks that the consequence of being hit is simply "being out of the game," and not "being shot dead." He thus conceptualizes his own and the others' behavior in terms of actual states of affairs, without any recourse to the imagination.

(2) Walter, however, could conceptualize the situation in a different way. As said, he could think of the action of "hitting with paint pellets" as "shooting to kill" and, when hit with a paint pellet, he could imagine that he has been "shot by an enemy." This conceptualization, Currie and Ravenscroft claim, is already a kind of pretense: Walter pretends to kill and to avoid being killed, by imagining that certain real events (firing with a toy-gun, being hit by a paint pellet, etc.) count as some other non-actual events (shooting at somebody, being shot and injured, etc.). Still, they say, his pretense does not need to be in a causal relation to his imaginative activity; in other words, it does not need to be motivated by his imagination. Walter could have, in fact, a genuine *desire to pretend* to kill someone, and a genuine belief that the best way to realize this desire, in his situation, is to hit the target subject with a paint pellet. In this case, then, it is his genuine desire (to pretend to kill), together with his genuine belief, which produces the action of shooting a person with paint pellets. No imagination is involved in the practical reasoning that guides his behavior (2002: 120).

(3) On the contrary, imagination can affect Walter's behavior – even if only in an indirect way – in the following scenario. Suppose that Walter is not only imagining that certain actions and events stand for other non-actual actions and events, but also that he wants to pretend in accordance to the contents of his imagination. For example, since he imagines that he has someone in the sights of his gun, he desires to pretend to shoot him; or, in consequence of imagining being shot, he desires to pretend to be injured (2002: 120). In these cases his imaginings at least have an influence on what he desires to pretend.

Moreover, Walter may also want to act in accordance to what he wishes to imagine in the future. For example, Walter may wish to imagine that he killed someone and this desire, together with the belief that the best way to pretend to shoot someone is to hit her with a paint pellet, could generate the desire to pretend to shoot someone. As it was in the previous case, also in this situation Walter's imaginings are not the direct cause of his behavior. The practical reasoning that motivates the pretender's behavior has been activated, again, by a genuine desire (the desire to imagine shooting someone), together with a genuine belief (the belief that this desire can be satisfied by shooting someone with paint pellets). Nevertheless, differently from the previous case, in this scenario Walter's imaginings have had an indirect influence on his behavior, since they have at least generated the desire to pretend to shoot someone (2002: 121).

(4) Imagination, Currie and Ravenscroft say, becomes the motivating aspect of pretense, only when the agent's behavior is directly caused by some

belief-like-imagining and some *desire-like imagining*, that is, by states that are the imaginative counterparts of some genuine belief and desire of ours. In other words, contrary to the previous scenario, in which Walter decides to engage in a certain behavior because of a genuine belief and a genuine desire, now his behavior is determined by a couple belief/desire that he has produced by help of his imagination. In this case, these philosophers observe (2002: 123) that we are dealing with "the most absorbed player," since his pretense is directly driven by the imagination, and he needs to deploy neither the concept of pretense, nor that of imagination. He does not desire to *pretend* to kill someone, but rather, he possesses a desire-like imagining to kill someone; he does not wish to *imagine* that he has been shot dead, but has a desire-like imagining of being shot dead.

In order to explain this point, Currie and Ravenscroft appeal to the distinction between *acting for the sake of* and *acting out of* something, and give the following example (2002: 122). Suppose that Mary and Jane are best friends. If Mary *acts for the sake of* her friendship with Jane, then she can decide, for example, to avoid saying something that could offend or hurt Jane, because she desires to preserve her friendship with her. Her behavior is thus motivated by a desire that contains the concept of *friendship* itself. On the contrary, if Mary *acts out of* her friendship with Jane, she simply decides to do something for her (e.g. organizing a trip with her) but the concept of *friendship* does not appear in her practical reasoning. In this case, then, Mary acts on the basis of a belief (for example, the belief that a trip could help Jane forget her ex-boyfriend) and of a desire (the desire that Jane feels better) that do contain the concept of friendship.

The same kind of distinction, Currie and Ravenscroft argue, holds between the third and the fourth case of pretense illustrated above. In the third scenario, Walter acts for *the sake of* his imagination. He pretends to shoot one of the players because he desires *imagining* that he has killed someone. This is the desire which motivates his behavior, thus containing the notion of *imagination*. On the contrary, in the latter scenario, the concept of imagination does not appear in the contents of the belief and the desire that motivate his behavior. Walter simply has a pretend desire to kill someone, and a pretend belief that the best way to reach this goal is to shoot somebody, so he *acts out of* his imaginings.

According to Currie and Ravenscroft, the roles played by imagination within pretense can thus be manifold. More precisely, imagination can be used for at least three different goals, namely: (1) to re-conceptualize what is happening in a certain context (as in the second scenario proposed); (2) to figure out certain possible scenarios, which can, in turn, give rise to some genuine desires to pretend in accordance to those imaginings (as in the third scenario); (3) to guide our behavior during pretense, by reproducing belief-like and desire-like imaginings (as in the last scenario). In this sense, it seems that we can distinguish among at least three different forms of pretense, depending on the kind of imaginings produced by the pretender and the role played by them within the cognitive architecture of the mind.

2.3. *Creative and recreative imagination*

In their book, *Recreative minds*, Currie and Ravenscroft distinguish between two fundamental kinds of imaginative abilities: *creative imagination* and *recreative imagination* (cf. 2002: 8-11).

More precisely, they define creative imagination as the ability to "put […] together ideas in a way that defies expectation or convention: the kind of imaginative 'leap' that leads to the creation of something valuable in art, science, or practical life" (2002: 9). In this sense, creative imagination is the capacity to produce something new and original, or innovative, in every possible field. On this account, the production of a ready-made by Duchamp, the invention of the prospective technique, or that of the telegraph should all be conceived as products of our creative imagination, since they do not rise from the mere imitation and reiteration of already-known rules and procedures. On the contrary, with the expression "recreative imagination," Currie and Ravenscroft mean the ability to reproduce in one's own mind the mental experiences one would undergo in a certain possible situation. A good example of what an episode of recreative imagination could be has been given by Kendall Walton (1997: 39):

Imagine going on a spelunking expedition. You lower yourself into a hole in the ground and enter a dank, winding passageway. After a couple of bends there is absolute pitch darkness. You light the carbide lamp on your helmet and continue. The passage narrows. You squeeze between the walls. After a while you have to stoop, and then crawl on your hands and knees. On and on, for hours, twisting and turning and descending. Your companion, following behind you, began the trip with enthusiasm and confidence; in fact she talked you into it. But you notice an increasingly nervous edge in her voice. Eventually, the ceiling gets too low even for crawling; you wriggle on your belly. Even so, there isn't room for the pack on your back. You slip it off, reach back, and tie it to your foot; then continue, dragging the back behind you. The passage bends sharply to the left, as it descend further. You contort your body, adjusting the angles of your shoulders and pelvis, and squeeze around and down. Now your companion is really panicked. Your lamp flickers a few times, then goes out. Absolute pitch darkness. You fumble with the mechanism…

As shown by this passage, imagining being trapped in a cave, several meters under the earth's surface, can be a complex experience, one which involves the production of a long series of different mental states. When reading these lines, we not only imagine being in a cave, but we also imagine being in nearly absolute darkness, in a cold, wet environment. We imagine our efforts crawling and squeezing ourselves into the cave, and most importantly, we can vividly imagine the increasing anxiety, the fear and finally the panic we would feel after realizing that we are lost and trapped in the cave. In a word, by means of our recreative imagination, we would be able to reproduce all the kinds of mental states that we would undergo, were we really in that possible situation. In this sense, Currie and Ravenscroft say (2002: 8-9), recreative imagination is nothing but *perspective-shifting*: "the capacity to put ourselves in the place of another, or in the place of our own future, past, or counterfactual self: seeing, thinking about, and responding to the world as the other sees, thinks about, and responds to it".

As regards the relationship between creative and recreative imagination, Currie and Ravenscroft also observe that, although creative imagination seems to depend, to a considerable extent, on the capacity for perspective-shifting – engaging with possible scenarios would enhance, in fact, our capacity to produce something new – there is no reason to deny the independence of these two abilities. Moreover, they appeal to Michael Tomasello (2000), according to whom apes are certainly creative beings, but they do not possess the capacity for imitative learning. Currie and Ravenscroft interpret his claim in terms of creative and recreative imagination. Apes would be capable of innovation – at least to some degree – and thus of creative thinking, but they would not be capable of learning something from others by understanding and reproducing their goals. For example, apes are able to find new manners to get some food (e.g. by using a cane to eat ants), but they cannot learn a new action from a conspecific, because they are not able to understand and reproduce the intention that has guided the action. Under the label "recreative imagination," Currie and Ravenscroft thus seem to understand the 'inner side' of what is sometimes called "emulation": the capacity to imitate a certain behavior in consequence of an inner imitation, that is, in consequence of having recreated in one's own mind the mental states that have guided a certain behavior (cf. e.g. Tennie, Call & Tomasello 2006).[10]

---

10   It is worth noting that the distinction between these two notions of imagination is not so different from the traditional distinction between the notion of *imaginatio* (the faculty to retain and reproduce what is absent) and *phantasia* (the faculty to

The distinction between creative and recreative imagination and, in particular, the conception of recreative imagination as a capacity for reproducing any kind of mental content is also directly tied to another important issue concerning the imagination, that is, the question of its alleged unity. Is imagination a single phenomenon or must we distinguish, under this label, different kinds of activities? As we will see in greater detail in the next two chapters, whereas the advocates of recreative imagination are typically committed to the thesis of the unity of imagination, those who treat imagination as a peculiar kind of mental state tend to make a distinction between, at least, "propositional imagination" on one side, and "sensory imagination" on the other.

3. *Mindreading*

As hinted above, a relevant part of the discussion about pretense is deeply intertwined with the investigation of another important capacity, usually called *folk psychology* or also *mindreading*[11]. This is defined as the capacity to understand and predict the behavior of other agents, as well as our own, by means of the ascription of mental states such as beliefs, desires, intentions, etc. For example, from the simple observation of a young child looking at a balloon seller, we can easily understand what she is *craving* and, from this, we can also guess her next move. That will probably consist of drawing mom's attention towards the balloons, in order to get one. But mindreading can be conducted also on our own behavior, as when we investigate what has led us to perform a certain action ("Why was I so rude with X?", "Am I angry with him, perhaps?"), or when we try to guess how we could react if faced with a certain situation ("What if X openly insulted me?").

Intuitively, the existence of a relation between pretense and mindreading seems to be quite an obvious fact. In order to pretend to be someone else, the pretender often needs to take the mental stance of the target subject, and thus needs to imagine what this subject would be inclined to do in that situation: that is, what the target subject would do *given her beliefs, desires,*

---

recombine, thus creating a new object). For a detailed discussion of the two notions cf. Ferraris 1996.

11   The term "mindreading" is used to mean, in particular, the capacity to understand others' minds and make *third-person* ascriptions, whereas the notion of "folk psychology" normally includes both *first person-* and *third person* mindreading. Sometimes the label "theory of mind" is also used as a synonym for "folk psychology," although this term is theoretically committed to a specific conception of our capacity to read minds, the so-called 'theory theory' of mindreading (cf. the next paragraph).

emotions, etc. The same holds if one imagines oneself in a certain possible situation. Pretending to be in a different situation often means to imagine what would be one's own state of mind in that situation, and how these states could possibly influence one's behavior (cf. also the examples given at the beginning of this chapter). On the other side, however, the relation between pretense and mindreading is all but clear. Although several correlational studies have confirmed that the two domains are certainly related (for a list cf. Lillard 2001: 496), the debate about the relation between these two skills is still very lively. Is some elementary form of mindreading required in order to pretend or, on the contrary, is pretense a necessary step in the development of a capacity for mindreading? Do they employ the same cognitive mechanisms? If so, what are these mechanisms?

Depending on the theory of mindreading adopted, different authors have offered different explanations for the kinds of mechanisms that would underlie pretense. For example, a "Metarepresentational Model"[12] like the one proposed by Leslie (1987) claims that pretense is an important step in the development of folk psychology, because during pretense children learn to manipulate mental representations, thus developing a metarepresentational capacity – a capacity for representing representations – that will be required, later, in order to understand others' minds. Other authors (cf. e.g. Harris 1995a, b; Goldman 2006b) have pointed, instead, to the importance of pretense in the development of a capacity for imagining "what it would be like to be in the other's shoes." By exercising this capacity in the context of pretense, they have argued, the child would progressively improve her capacity for simulating the mental states entertained by other people, thus rapidly coming to understand what another person could think and feel in a certain possible situation.

In what follows, we will sum up the fundamental issues that characterize the debate about the nature of mindreading, focusing in particular on two different kinds of simulation that are supposed to be at the basis of our capacity for pretending. Finally, we will take into consideration the relationship existing between imagination and simulation – a relationship that has apparently evolved from initial distinction to nearly complete identification.

3.1. *Theory-theory vs. simulation theory*

The capacity for mindreading has first been explained by appealing to a theory – a "theory of the mind" – that is, to a body of knowledge concern-

---

12   This label is due to Lillard 2001.

ing the psychological domain, on which one could operate by means of her own inferential mechanisms in order to produce some causal explanation of a certain behavior.[13] For example, I could possess, stored in my mind, a certain piece of information of the kind: "If a subject wants that p, and she knows that, in order to obtain p, it is necessary to do x, *ceteris paribus*, she will do x." Relying on this piece of knowledge, with the help of my inference mechanisms, I could then reason about singular cases. For example, if I know that Giulia desires to eat candy and she knows that she can find some in my bag, by relying on the general rule illustrated above, I can easily infer that she will rummage through my bag in order to get candy. Or, vice versa, if I notice that Giulia is rummaging through my bag and I know that she knows that she can find candy there, then I will immediately infer that she desires candy. Our theory of mind could thus be used both to predict someone's behavior, starting from her mental states, or to guess the mental states that have caused a certain behavior.

Although all "theory-theorists" agree on the fact that our capacity for mindreading is theoretical in its nature[14], we can still find enormous differences in the way they conceive this theory. For example, the psychologists Alison Gopnik and Andrew Meltzoff (1997) have claimed that our theory of mind would consist of something analogous to a scientific theory – a theory that children acquire through their experience of the world, and that they revise several times during their development, adjusting it to new evidence, which they collect time after time. This explanation, however, has received some severe criticisms. First, because it implies that the child would have always a conscious access to her theory of mind – a fact that seems all but obvious. Second, and more importantly, this is because it cannot avoid the typical objection from the "stimulus error argument": if children should really build their theory of mind upon their experience of the word, by trial-and-error, then we should find important differences among the theories that they formulate individually. On the contrary, what we observe is that the capacity for mindreading is acquired through some fixed steps in every child with normal development, from the emergence of

---

13 That is why the term 'theory of mind' is often used as a synonymous of 'mindreading'. This identification, however, is not completely correct, since with 'mindreading' we mean a certain capacity (the capacity to attribute mental states to other people and to predict their behavior on the basis of this attribution), whereas with the term 'theory of mind' we rather mean the nature of this capacity, which, according to some philosophers and psychologists, would consist, as said, in the possession of a theory.

14 The term 'Theory theory' is thus used as opposed to 'Simulation theory'.

the capacity for attributing intentions to other people at around 6 months, to the complex capacity to attribute false beliefs between the 3rd and the 4th year (cf. Baron-Cohen, Leslie & Frith 1995).

By relying on this developmental data, other psychologists (Baron-Cohen, Leslie & Frith 1995; Baron-Cohen 1995) have thus proposed a different hypothesis on the nature of mindreading. They have argued, more precisely, that our theory of mind would need to rely on a module or, better, a group of modules[15] dedicated to processing different social stimuli and to producing representations of states of mind of growing complexity.

For example, if we follow the most famous system for mindreading, proposed by Baron-Cohen (1995), we can distinguish among at least 4 specialized modules. The first, called EDD (*Eye Direction Detector*), emerging already in the first months of life, is devoted to the computation of the gaze direction, thus producing representations of the form "X *sees* Y". Then, by the age of 6 months, a more complicated mechanism, ID (*Intentionality Detector*), allows the children to attribute basic volitional states (goals). Starting from the observation of other people's behavior, it constructs representations of the form "X *has-for-goal* Y". For example, from observing her father going towards a cake, the infant would be able to understand that her father has-for-goal the cake. Later, the child learns to compute the dyadic representations coming from both EDD and ID – which are representations of a binary relation, between the agent and an object – and to construct more complicated representations – representations of triadic relations, between an agent, another agent and an object. By observing the gaze of another person, which is directed to an object, the infant would be able, in other words, to form some triadic representations of the kind: "I *seeing* (agent *seeing* object)" and, conversely, "agent *seeing* (me *seeing* object)". This module, emerging at around 9 months, is called SAM (*Shared Attention Mechanism*), precisely because it is the mechanism that allows the child to understand a state of shared attention. Finally, at around the age of 18 months, the child would acquire the most complicated mechanism, TOMM (the *Theory of Mind Mechanism*), which allows the infant to construct 4-places representations: that is, representation concerning an agent, an informational relation entertained by the agent, a primary representation (a representation of reality) and a secondary representation (a representation of a state-of-affairs within an intensional context)[16]. For example, the

---

15   The notion of 'module' employed by these authors is the Fodorian one (cf. Fodor 1983).

16   We will come back to this point in chapter 4 (cf. §§ 1.1-1.2).

child would be able to construct the representation: "Mom (the agent) pretends (the informational relation), of the banana (primary representation), that it is a telephone (secondary representation)".

On this account, then, our theory of mind would consist in a domain-specific knowledge, to which the subject has no conscious access and that is automatically produced every time the subject encounters certain kinds of stimuli.

Since the second half of the '80s, however, a new paradigm has emerged. In contrast with the theory-theorists, the so-called "Simulation theorists" of mindreading (Gordon 1986; Heal 1986; Goldman 1989; Harris 1989, 1995a) have claimed that the theory-theory approach cannot satisfactorily account for the rapidity and spontaneity of our mental states attributions. In other words, if every time I wanted to understand or predict another's behavior, I should appeal to some theory of the mind and make use of my inferential mechanisms, this task would take me a relatively long time and would not be so easily carried out.[17] But this contrasts with the immediateness and spontaneity that we all experience in understanding an observed behavior.[18] As it is often said, when we look at somebody, we have the impression to perceive her mental states – the beliefs and desires which underlie her actions – in the same manner we perceive the color of her eyes, her actions, or the expressions on her face (cf. Dennett 1987: 21).

The simulation theorists have thus claimed that our capacity for mindreading should be conceived, rather than as a theory, as a heuristics. That is,

---

17　This criticism is valid only against the first form of theory of mind that we have taken into consideration, that is, the hypothesis of the child-as-scientist, but does not apply, instead, to a modular theory of mind, since the latter is supposed to work at a subpersonal level and to compute the stimuli in a completely automatic way.

18　An example that has been frequently used by the simulation theorists against the theory-theorists is the following story, ideated by Kahneman and Tversky (1982): "Mr. Crane and Mr. Tees were scheduled to leave the airport on different flights, at the same time. They travelled from town in the same limousine, were caught in a traffic jam, and arrived at the airport 30 minutes after the scheduled departure time of their flights. Mr. Crane is told that his flight left on time. Mr. Tees is told that his flight was delayed, and just left five minutes ago. Who is more upset, Mr. Crane or Mr. Tees?" 96% of the subjects interviewed by Kahneman and Tversky answered that the more upset would have been certainly Mr. Tees. Now, if we should recur to some kind of theory in order to understand Mr. Crane and Mr. Tees' states of mind, the simulationist theorists have argued, we should make appeal to a great amount of knowledge and our answers could not be so quick and sure as they are. The only plausible possibility, the simulationists have thus concluded, is that the subjects simply take the part of Mr. Crane and Mr. Tees, thus simulating their states of mind.

as a practical ability to put oneself in one's shoes, to simulate the thoughts and feelings one would undergo if she were in a certain possible situation. A good example has been given by Gordon (1986/1995: 63). When I play chess, he says, and I have to predict my opponent's next move, what I do is simply pretend to be him. I put myself, imaginatively, in his situation and I decide which move is best in that situation; then, I simply have to ascribe my decision to him. A similar procedure can also be employed for a retrodictive task: for example, if my opponent makes an unexpected move, I can infer that she is applying a different strategy and so, I have to imagine which antecedent states could have led me to adopt such a strategy and to make such a move.

The typical simulative heuristics can thus be summed up in the following three steps:

(1) first of all, we have to assume – physically, or whenever this is not possible, in our own imagination – the perspective of a certain subject, that is we have to imagine the situation she is in and what she would think, desire, and feel in that situation;

(2) then, we can feed our own cognitive mechanisms with these mental states and let them run *off-line*, that is: let them work on these pretend inputs as if they worked on our own mental states;

(3) finally, we can ascribe the output of this process – i.e. the result of this computation performed on pretend inputs – to the subject who is the target of our simulation process.

The general idea of simulation is that since all human beings are provided with the same cognitive mechanisms, once I have assumed the perspective of a certain subject, I can make use of my own cognitive mechanisms in order to understand what is going on in the other's mind, and anticipate her or his behavior. In this sense, for a simulationist, the idea that we can put ourselves in the other's shoes is much more than a metaphor. We can literally put ourselves – at the cognitive and, presumably, neural level – in the other's mind.

As we will see in the next paragraph, however, the simulation theory of mindreading has also received some important criticisms. In particular, it has been claimed that the simulationist account can perhaps explain one part, but not the entire process of mindreading, since it cannot explain how, exactly, we can *recognize the outputs* of the simulation process, in order to attribute them to the target subject. As seen, once the simulation has run, the outputs of the process must be identified as certain kinds of mental states before being attributed to the target. For example, let us suppose that I want to understand how my friend would react if he woke up in the middle of the night and suspected that there is a burglar in his home. If I simulate having a certain belief (the belief that there is a burglar in the house) and a certain desire (the desire to be protected), after reasoning on these pretend inputs, I will come up with the conclusion that it would be better to call the police. Before attributing this state to my friend, however, I must identify this output as a certain kind of state – that is, as an *intention* to call the police. Moreover, I must identify this state as a *pretend* intention, rather than a genuine one, otherwise it would lead me to act accordingly, thus with me calling the police.

Depending on the way the simulation theorists have tried to give an answer to these problems, we can distinguish two different kinds of simulation: a "moderate" form of simulation, whose principal proponent has been the philosopher Alvin Goldman (1989), who has recognized the necessity of a theory in addition to the simulative process; and a "radical" form of simulation, proposed by the philosopher Robert Gordon (1986), who excludes, instead, the intervention of any theory within the process of mindreading.

3.2. *Moderate simulation*

The moderate version of the simulation theory of mindreading, famously proposed by Goldman (1989, 1993, 2006b), is certainly the one which has received the widest consensus, due to the fact that it can easily explain a great amount of data without incurring those kinds of problems that, as we will see in the next paragraph, afflict instead the radical version proposed by Gordon. As anticipated, this conception is moderate insofar as it recognizes the intervention of a minimal core of theory at different stages in the process of simulation. More precisely, Goldman concedes that we can make appeal to a minimal amount of theory, both at the beginning and at the end of the simulative process, that is, both before and after the simulative process has run.

On the one hand, in fact, it is possible that some theoretic knowledge guides my imagination in figuring out the mental states entertained by the target subject in a certain situation. For example, if I have to imagine how my friend would behave during his first international congress of philosophy, I must have some knowledge of what an international congress of philosophy is and what you are supposed to do at such a congress. Relying on my experience of previous congresses, I could thus *imagine myself in that situation* and, by a simple *inference from me to you*, determine what the other might think and feel in that situation. This knowledge, however, is often insufficient. How my friend will behave during his first international congress certainly also depends on his nature, that is, on whether he is self-confident, whether he feels comfortable speaking a foreign language, whether he has already experienced analogous situations, and so on. In order to come to an adequate prediction, then, a considerable amount of knowledge must be taken into consideration before running the simulation process.

On the other hand, as anticipated above (cf. the end of § 3.1), once the simulation has run, a theory seems to be required in order to recognize the kinds of mental states that result from the simulation process. In other words, how can I tell whether the result of my simulation is a *belief*, an *intention*, or an *emotion*?

According to Goldman, the simulation process necessarily requires a subsequent phase of *introspection*, one by means of which the simulator focuses on her inner state and comes to recognize it as a certain kind of mental state (a belief, a desire, an intention, etc.). This phase of introspection, however, is precisely what has been most frequently criticized in Goldman's account. Goldman (1993) initially thought of introspection as consisting in the recognition of some phenomenological property of the state. In other words, according to him every kind of mental state would have been characterized by a distinctive *quale*, which the simulator would have been able to recognize. This solution, however, has been widely criticized, since it is difficult to think that there is a different *quale* for every kind of mental state. In particular, what would be the peculiar *quale* of a belief? What would it be like, for example, to believe that "there are no kangaroos on Mars", or that "2+2=4"?[19]

Later, Goldman abandoned this solution and opted for a different explanation, which appeals to a possible matching between the neural properties of a given mental state *token,* and those which are characteristic of a certain mental state *type* (cf. 2006b: ch. 7). In other words, Goldman claims that every kind of mental state would be characterized by a specific neural pattern, so that, when an occurrent mental state matches that pattern, it is recognized – at a personal level – as a certain kind of state: a belief, a desire, an intention, etc. This solution, however, does not seem to be more plausible than the previous one since, given the experimental evidence at disposal, we are far from having identified something like the neural correlates of our mental states *types* and it is not clear at all whether these correlates really exist. Moreover, it is quite difficult to understand

---

19   On this point cf. e.g. Meini 2001: 29-31.

how a mere neural matching could give rise to the explicit identification of a certain mental state type which is required by mindreading.

Moreover, even if we were able to identify these neural correlates, and Goldman's theory turned out to be true, one problem would stay unsolved. The problem with the identification of the mental state produced by the simulation process, in fact, is not confined to the individuation of its *type*, but it also concerns the identification of this state as a *pretend* mental state. In other words, the subject must not only recognize the simulated mental state as a certain type of state, but she must also keep it separate from her genuine states. As we will see in detail in chapter 2, this is a problem which afflicts every simulation theory of the imagination, that is, every theory which conceives of imagination as a capacity for reproducing different kinds of mental states.

3.3. *Radical simulation*

As hinted before, the kind of simulation proposed by Gordon has been defined as a "radical" one, since it excludes from the simulation process – at any stage, from the moment of perspective taking to the attribution of the simulated mental state – the use of mental concepts such as 'belief,' 'desire,' 'intention,' etc. In Gordon's view, in fact, every appeal to these concepts would necessarily imply leaving a door open for the intervention of a theory, and this is precisely what Gordon rejects. For him mindreading is simply a matter of applying a heuristics, not of possessing a theory. More precisely, Gordon conceives the process of simulation as a *transformation*, rather than as a mere *transfer* (1995: 54). Contrary to Goldman, according to whom I would first have to imagine what *I* would think and how *I* would feel in a certain possible situation (although, as seen, with the 'adjustments' required by the case), and only then could I attribute my states to the target subject, Gordon thinks of the simulation process as an act of personal transformation, by means of which I can literally become another subject, thus representing things from her point of view, not from mine. In order to illustrate this point, Gordon (1995: *ibidem*) appeals to the Tees/Crane example (cf. footnote 18), which says that when I have to find out how Mr. Tees feels in his situation, I do not imagine how I would feel in Tees' situation, but rather, "I have the option of imaging in the first person Mr. Tees barely missing his flight, rather than imaging myself, a particular individual distinct from Mr. Tees, in such a situation and then extrapolating to Mr. Tees." (1995: 55) Consequently, I, the simulating subject, cease to be the referent of "I" and "I" refers, instead, to Mr. Tees.

In this sense, then, contrary to Goldman, the kind of simulation proposed by Gordon seems to require neither introspection nor an inference
"from me to you," but rather an "egocentric shift" (1995: 54):

> [...] once a personal transformation has been accomplished, there is no remain-
> ing task of mentally *transferring* a state from one person to another, no question of
> *comparing* Mr Tees to myself. For insofar as I have recentered my egocentric map
> on Mr Tees, I am not considering what RMG [Robert M. Gordon, N/A] would do,
> think, want, and feel in the situation. Within the context of the simulation, RMG is
> out of the picture altogether. In short, when I simulate Mr Tees missing his flight, I
> am already representing him as having been in a certain state of mind.

Now, this personal transformation, when combined with a special heuristics – what Gordon calls the *ascent routine* (1986; 1995) – can explain
our capacity of mindreading.

Let us first consider the case of beliefs attribution. According to Gordon,
when we have to answer a question about our own beliefs – for example,
when we have to answer the question: "Do you believe that Italians like
pizza?" – we do not interrogate ourselves about our actual beliefs, but rather go down one level and answer a simpler question about a certain state of
affairs like "do Italians like pizza?" Once we have given an answer to this
lower-level question, all we have to do is to put it into a more complicated
syntactical structure of the type: "Yes (No), I do (not) believe that Italians like pizza". In other words, in Gordon's account the self-ascription of
beliefs does not necessarily require that we possess and apply the mental
concept of 'belief,' but it only requires that we are able to deal with certain
syntactical structures: every time we encounter a syntactical structure of
the kind "do you believe that *p*?", all we have to do is to answer the lower-
level question "*p*?", and then put the answer within a higher-level structure
of the kind: "Yes, I do believe that___" or "no, I do not believe that___".

Things go much the same way for third-person attributions. For example, when we have to answer a question about the mental state entertained
by another person, such as: "Does Mary believe that tomorrow will be a
sunny day?", what we have to do is not to reason about her beliefs, but
again, only about a certain state of affairs. The only difference is that, in
this case, we have to first change our perspective, i.e. we have to assume
Mary's perspective, to transform ourselves into Mary. Once the personal
transformation has occurred, again, we can go down one level and answer
the simpler question, "Will tomorrow be a sunny day?", as if we were
Mary. Finally, we fit the answer into the higher-level syntactical scheme:
"Yes (No), Mary does (not) believe that___". On Gordon's account, then,

third-person mindreading works exactly as first-person mindreading does, with the only addition of a phase of personal transformation.

A problem with this strategy, however, is that it works well only in the case of beliefs, but not for other types of mental states (cf. Meini 2001: 37). For example, if I have to answer the question "Does Mary want tomorrow to be a sunny day?", answering the lower-level question "Will tomorrow be a sunny day?" will not be of any help to give an answer to the first question. This is true for other states as well, such as emotions, intentions, etc. In other words, in cases different from belief, it seems to be absolutely necessary for us to reason about the subject's mental states – and consequently, to make use of some mental concepts – if we want to understand and predict her behavior.

Even more problematic is the notion of "personal transformation." As stressed by Meini and Voltolini (2010: 53), in fact, the kind of simulation envisaged by Gordon requires a deep change in the simulator's personality. The subject must stop being herself and become someone else but, as the authors rightly remark, this seems to be too much, even for a good actor of the Stanislavskij method. What Gordon prospects, in other words, seems to be metaphysically impossible. As we know, identity is not among those properties that can be acquired or lost at will, so it is not possible to transform oneself, literally, into another individual. But if the personal transformation is not this, what else can it be? Finally, even if the personal transformation envisaged by Gordon were possible, a subject who underwent a simulative process would be, in the end, a hallucinating person. That means that the case of someone who simulated to be Napoleon would not be distinguishable from the case of someone who really believed to be Napoleon, since in both cases we would deal with someone who believes to be someone else. On the contrary, what a simulative process seems to presuppose is precisely that the simulator maintains her own identity, even if she reproduces certain mental states, which are not genuine states of hers.

These problems explain why there is not much consensus behind the theory proposed by Gordon. In the fifth chapter, we will come back to this issue and try to explain how the notion of a "personal transformation" can be reinterpreted within a relativist framework so as to avoid the problems afflicting Gordon's theory.

3.4. *Imagination and simulation*

From the picture of simulation sketched above (cf. § 3.1), it seems correct to infer that simulation and imagination were originally conceived as quite separate abilities. On the one hand, in fact, imagination would have been required in order to produce the pretend mental states that constitute the inputs to the simulative process, whereas this latter would have consisted in making certain cognitive mechanisms run on these pretend states as if they operated on some genuine states of ours.

Recently, however, this picture has started to change, in particular after the hypotheses advanced by Currie and Ravenscroft. In two seminal papers (cf. Currie 1995; Currie & Ravenscroft 1997), they have first proposed to extend the concept of simulation to the field of sensory imagination, claiming that at least some forms of imagery[20] (visual and motor imagery) can be considered as typical instances of a simulative process. As we will see in more detail in chapter 2, their idea is that, similarly to the classical model of simulation sketched above, also in the cases of visual and motor imagery, the mechanisms which are usually employed, respectively, in visual perception and motor planning can also be recruited for the imagination of certain visual scenes or to imagine the execution of certain movements. In other words, the same cognitive mechanisms that are at the basis of vision and movement would be employed *off-line* in order to realize a different function: to imagine something. Imagery has thus ended by clashing, in their account, with the process of simulation itself or, at least, with the output of this process.

This proposal has been later extended from basic states as perceptions and motor plans to higher-order mental states, such as beliefs and desires (Currie & Ravenscroft 2002). By means of a simulation process, It has been argued, in fact, that by means of a simulation process we would be able to reproduce *belief-like* and *desire-like imaginings*, i.e. states of mind that possess exactly the same internal functional roles that characterize genuine beliefs and desires. An analogous thesis has also been sustained by Goldman (2006a, b), who has opposed to the classical conception of propositional imagination as an act of purely conceptual imagination, lacking any sensory aspect, a new conception of the imagination as an *enactive* activity (*Enactment-imagination*), "a matter of creating or trying to create in one's own mind a selected mental state, or at least a rough facsimile of such a state" (2006a: 42). Typical examples of Enactment-imagination, Goldman says, are all sensory forms of imagination, such as visual or tac-

---

20   On the notion of imagery and its difference with cognitive imagination cf. the entry "Imagination" on the Stanford Encyclopedia of Philosophy (http://plato.stanford.edu/entries/imagination/). Briefly, whereas *imagery* or *sensory imagination* would consist of "forming a mental image" of something, *cognitive imagination* would rather consist of "conceptually entertaining a possibility."

tile imagination, by which the subject reproduces perception-like states, but also supposing that *p*, he claims, can be conceived as the "enaction" of a belief with content *p* (2006a: *ibidem*).

As one can easily see then, the notion of imagination has ended up collapsing that of simulation. If visual imagination can be conceived as the simulation of vision, and motor imagination as the simulation of a motor plan, propositional imagination is nothing but the simulation of belief (Goldman 2006a). In this sense, Currie and Ravenscroft (2002) have spoken of our minds as *recreative minds*. Minds, that is, which are characterized by the peculiar capacity to reproduce different kinds of mental states and processes also in the absence of those stimuli which are typically responsible for the formation of a certain thought, or the activation of a certain cognitive mechanism.

Summary of the chapter

In this chapter we have made a preliminary analysis of three concepts: pretense, imagination and mindreading. In particular, what we have tried to do is to outline the most relevant relations among these three notions. In the next chapter, we will focus on the notion of a pretend mental state and contrast two different theories: the one proposed by Nichols and Stich, in the context of a wider explanation of our capacity for pretending (2000), and the one proposed by Goldman (2006a, b) and Currie and Ravenscroft (2002). As we will try to show, both theories encounter some problems tied to the need to define the special nature of a "pretend mental state."

II.
THE NATURE OF A PRETEND MENTAL STATE

In the first chapter, we have discussed the importance that imagination and mindreading have in the process of engaging in and understanding an episode of pretense. In this chapter, we will focus on the former capacity and analyze in detail two competing theories of the imagination, which imply two different conceptions of a "pretend mental state."

On one side, the theory of imagination proposed by Nichols and Stich (2000) conceives our imaginings as a special type of mental states, characterized by a peculiar functional role within the mind, different from those characterizing beliefs, desires, perceptions etc. On the other side, the 'recreativist' theories proposed by Mulligan (1999), Currie and Ravenscroft (2002) and Goldman (2006a, b) understand imagination as a heuristics, by means of which we would be able to reproduce every kind of mental state, thus re-instantiating in our mind belief-like states, desire-like states, vision-like states, and so on. These states, in turn, could guide our behavior during pretense in exactly the same way as our genuine states do.

In what follows, we will discuss in detail the cognitive architectures which are presupposed by these two opposed conceptions of the imagination as well as the peculiar problems affecting each theory, and we will finally show that both approaches, in this respect, are quite unsatisfying.[1]

1. Imagination as a mental state type

One of the most well-known accounts of pretense is certainly the "cognitive theory of pretense" – as the authors themselves, Nichols and Stich

---

1   For the moment we will not take into consideration, instead, the famous account of pretense proposed by Leslie (1987, 1994). The reason is that Leslie's theory of pretense does not imply an especially interesting theory of the imagination *per se*. Rather, the peculiarity of Leslie's theory is the metarepresentational ability that Leslie presupposes in order to explain how we can link our primary representations (representations of real states-of-affairs) with our decoupled representations (representations of imaginary states-of-affairs) during an episode of pretense. Leslie's theory will be thus discussed in chapter 4, when we will be concerned with the metarepresentational abilities that are required by pretense.

(2000), have defined it. In § I.1.3 we have analyzed the features which, according to Nichols and Stich, characterize a typical episode of pretense: the initial premise, the inferential and non-inferential elaboration of the contents of pretense, the cognitive quarantine of the imaginative states, and the behavior that people assume in accordance to their imaginings. Here I will consider in more detail the architecture of the mind that Nichols and Stich have designed in order to account for all these features, paying particular attention to the place they have assigned to our imaginings. The section will thus develop as follows. I will start by illustrating the architecture of the mind initially adopted by Nichols and Stich (§ 1.1). Then, I will focus on the changes that they have introduced in this architecture in order to account for pretense (§ 1.2). Finally, I will try to highlight the kinds of problems that afflict this conception of the mind (§§ 1.3-1.4).

1.1. *The original architecture of the mind*

The cognitive architecture of the mind elaborated by Nichols and Stich (2000) to explain pretense constitutes an updated version of a previous picture of the mind, designed by the same authors in 1992, which has become very popular among cognitive scientists. According to Stich and Nichols (1992), the mind can be represented as a collection of boxes, all connected to one another.[2] Some of them represent different types of cognitive mechanisms, such as the Decision-making system, the Body monitoring system, the Action control systems, and so on; others stand for different types of mental states such as beliefs, desires, intentions etc. (cf. fig. 1: squared boxes stand for different types of mental states, whereas cognitive mechanisms are represented by hexagonal boxes).

---

2   The idea that our mind could be described as a collection of boxes, defined in functional terms was introduced for the first time by Stephen Schiffer (1981).

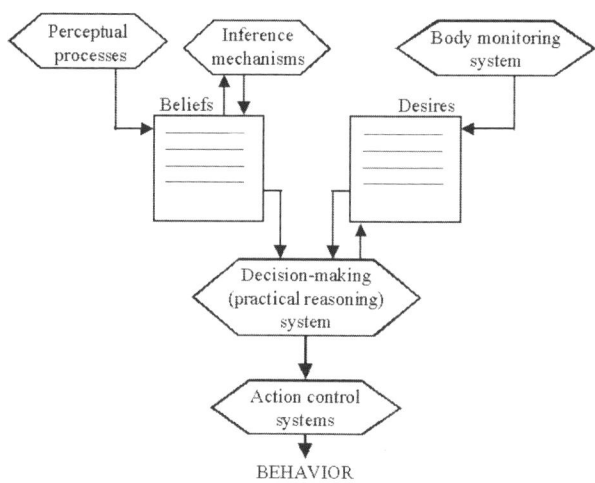

Figure 1

Within this picture of the mind, then, every box stands for a certain *type* of mental entity – be it a computational mechanism or a mental state – and is defined by the totality of the *functional relations* it entertains with other mental states and mechanisms. For example, the Decision-making system is a mechanism related, on the one hand, with the Belief Box and the Desire Box (from which it takes its inputs) and, on the other hand, with the Action control systems (to which it usually delivers its outputs). Much the same way, beliefs can be defined as states produced either by our perceptual processes or by our inference mechanisms, and constitute, together with desires, the typical inputs for the Decision-making system (cf. fig. 1).

Given this picture of the mind, it follows that the different types of mental states can be distinguished not in virtue of their *content*, but rather, in virtue of the *functional role* they play within the mind. For example, a belief and a desire can well share the same content – I can believe that "tomorrow I will have a party", but I can desire this as well – but they have different functional roles[3]: while the belief that "tomorrow Susan will give a party" is a piece of information that I have at disposal, to which I must adapt my behavior (for example, by buying a gift), the desire that "today

---

3   In 'boxological' terms this means that the same propositional content p (e.g. "tomorrow Susan will give a party") can appear, at the same time, in two different boxes (i.e. the Belief Box and the Desire Box).

Susan will have a party" is something I hope will become true, and thus drives my behavior in a different way (so as to realize this possible scenario, for example, I would try to convince Susan to give a party). The simulation theorists of mindreading have also employed this cognitive architecture. As we have seen, the general idea of simulation is that, when we simulate, we make use of some of our own cognitive mechanisms *off-line*. That means that we make them work independently of their standard inputs and, by feeding them with some *pretend states*, we obtain outputs relatively similar to those we would have obtained if we had made them work on our genuine representations.

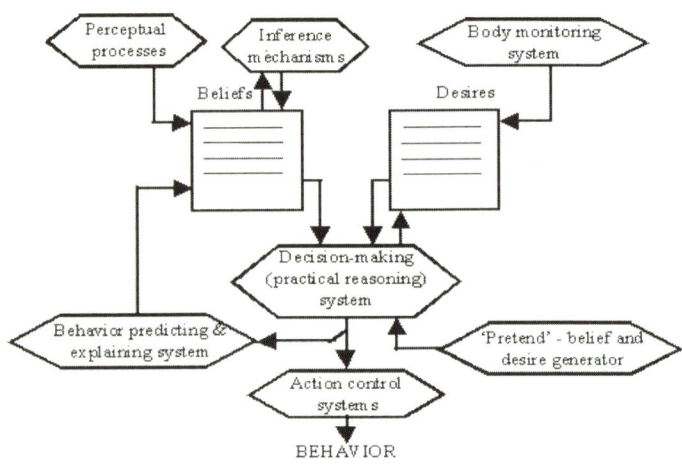

Figure 2

For example, in the typical case, we feed our Decision-making system with a couple belief/desire generated by a dedicated mechanism, the "Pretend belief and desire generator" (cf. fig. 2). These pretend inputs are then computed by our Decision-making system *as if* they were genuine states of ours, thus producing an output which is similar, in important respects, to the output that this mechanism would have generated, had it been fed with genuine beliefs and desires of ours. During mindreading, however, this output is not given – as it usually is – to the Action control systems, but it is rather deviated to a system dedicated to the prediction and explanation of someone's behavior (the "Behavior predicting and explaining system", cf. fig. 2).

Coming to pretense, one could argue that the same cognitive architecture employed for simulation can also be exploited during a game of make-believe. When we pretend, in fact, we conform our behavior to some imaginary representations, which are treated by our cognitive mechanisms *as if* they were the representations of some actual states of affairs. For example, an imaginary representation of the cup in front of me having been filled with some tea and then being turned upside down would lead me to imagine that the tea has been poured on the table and to pretend, accordingly, to dry the table. In this sense, Nichols and Stich say (2000: 131), pretense can be interpreted as a case of *on-line* simulation: a mental simulation whose output is not attributed – as it usually is – to another subject (through the Behavior-predicting and explaining system), but it is rather transmitted to the Action control systems, thus giving rise to some overt behavior. According to Nichols and Stich (2000), however, the picture of the mind adopted by the simulation theory of mindreading is not sufficient in order to explain pretense. More precisely, there are at least two major problems that arise within this paradigm.

The first concerns the phenomenon of *cognitive quarantine*. As we have seen (cf. § I.1.3), a person who is truly pretending is capable of keeping her pretend representations distinct from her genuine beliefs and desires, so that she will not think, in consequence of having pretended to pour some water on the table, that the table has really become wet. Pretend events have consequences only within pretense, not in real life. But the simulationist account of pretense, Nichols and Stich claim, cannot explain how this is possible, meaning how it is that we keep our pretend representations distinct from our genuine beliefs.

According to simulation theory, in fact – at least to the version proposed by Gordon and Baker (1994: cf. esp. p. 172) –, in the course of a game of make-believe, a pretend representation (corresponding to what Nichols and Stich call "the initial premise") is added to one's own genuine representations of the actual world (the Belief Box), thus becoming a possible input for some cognitive mechanisms of ours. For example, if a premise with content "The cup has been filled with some tea" is added to the set of beliefs possessed by the subject, and then the cup is turned upside down, the subject will come to the conclusion that the tea has been poured and that the cup is now empty. This happens, according to the authors, because the imaginary representation ("The cup has been filled with some tea") is given as input to our inference mechanisms, together with some of our other beliefs (e.g. "The cup has been turned upside down", "If you turn a cup upside down, its liquid will be poured"). The pretend representations resulting from this computation ("The cup has been poured", "The cup is empty", "The table is dry" etc.) are then added to the Belief Box, thus enriching the sets of beliefs entertained by the subject. The problem, however, is that Gordon and Barker do not explain why these pretend representations have no effect on our behavior outside pretense. In other words, how is it that we do not look for a cloth in order to wipe the table, if there is a representation with content "The table is wet" in our Belief Box?[4] And, moreover, how can we avoid confusion if, on the one hand, we genuinely believe that the table is dry but, on the other hand, we have a pretend belief that it is wet?

The second difficulty, according to Nichols and Stich (2000: 134), consists in the fact that simulation theory fails to explain the pretender's motivation to perform the actions she performs during the pretense (e.g. the fact that the child pretends to drink some tea from an empty cup, or to speak with her grandma holding a banana in her hand). According to simulation theory, in fact, the pretender would be capable of reproducing, by help of the imagination, not only a state that resembles, in important respects, a belief of hers, but also a desire-like representation. In other words, not only a pretend belief would be added to the Belief Box (e.g. the belief that "there is some tea in the cup"), but also the Desire Box would acquire a new, imaginary desire (e.g. a desire with the content "I drink the tea"). Only these two states together, when given to the Decision-making system, would be capable of producing a decision that could motivate the pretender's behavior.

This solution, however, poses two main problems in Nichols and Stich's opinion. First, if we suppose that pretend desires – analogously to pretend beliefs – possess the same causal power possessed by their genuine counterparts, then we should expect the pretender to show exactly the same behavior she would show in an analogous, but real situation. In other words, if the pretender is capable of reproducing imaginary desires, along with imaginary beliefs, how can we then explain the existence of certain systematic differences between her pretend and real behaviors (e.g. the fact that the child only pretends to eat the muddy cake but does not really do it,

---

4   Of course, I could decide to behave in accordance with what I am pretending, and
     then I could decide to pretend to wipe the table. But in this case I would not be
     confusing my representations of the actual world and the representations of the
     pretense world. I would be simply acting in accordance with my pretend representations rather than with my genuine beliefs.

whereas she does not hesitate when dealing with a real chocolate cake)? If we suppose that the pretender possesses both a pretend belief and a pretend desire, with the same functional roles characterizing their genuine counterparts, we should expect the pretender to exhibit exactly the same behavior she would exhibit in a corresponding, real situation (2000: *ibidem*).[5]

In the second place, Nichols and Stich argue, some pretend behaviors simply cannot be explained by appealing to pretend beliefs and desires. For example, dead cats do not have desires (nor they have beliefs), so it seems that, when a subject pretends to be a dead cat, she must appeal to something different than a pretend desire, in order to adopt the appropriate behavior. Rather, Nichols and Stich say (2000: *ibidem*),

> the Pretense Box has a representation with the content *This* [my body] *is a dead cat*, along with some additional representations about what the dead cat looks like. And what leads the pretender to do what she does is not some bizarre desire that might be attributed to a dead cat, but simply a quite real desire to 'behave' in a way that is similar to the way a dead cat described in the Pretense Box would behave.

To sum up, the architecture of the mind presupposed by the simulation theory of mindreading, Stich and Nichols (1992) claim, is insufficient in explaining pretense. As we will see in the next paragraph, some adjustments are needed. In particular, Nichols and Stich stress the importance of recognizing the specific nature of a pretend mental state and its place within the cognitive architecture of the mind. Within the discussion about mindreading, this notion was left quite unspecified: the idea was simply that, when we want to understand or predict someone's behavior, we have to produce, by the help of the imagination, some pretend mental states, and the more these states resemble their genuine counterparts, the more the simulation process will succeed. No hint, however, was given about the functional role played by these states and their specific causal powers within the mind.

1.2. *Cognitive mechanisms underlying pretense*

In more recent years, Nichols and Stich (2000) have tried to specify the nature of our pretend mental states, and this has led them to modify their own cognitive architecture of the mind.

---

5   I will come back to this issue in chapter 3, as I will discuss in more detail the debate concerning the existence of pretend desires.

First, pretend mental states have been recognized as a special kind of mental state and, more precisely, as that type of state whose "[...] job is not to represent the world as it is or as we'd like it to be, but rather to represent what the world would be like given some set of assumptions that we may neither believe to be true nor want to be true" (2000: 122). A "Pretense box" or "Possible Worlds Box" (from now on, PWB) has thus been added to their picture of the mind, in order to stress the specificity of our pretend representations (that the authors call *suppositions*) which would be characterized by a *specific functional role*, distinct from those of beliefs and desires (cf. fig. 3)[6].

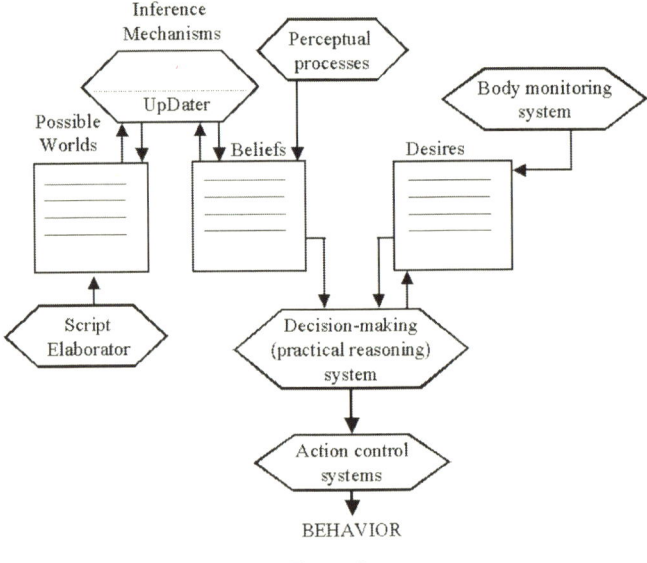

Figure 3

In other words, although pretend mental states admittedly share several features with genuine beliefs (e.g. they are treated in the same manner by some cognitive mechanisms such as the inference mechanisms or the Decision-making system), they also show some functional peculiarities.

---

6   It is worth noting that the PWB is thus involved not only in pretense, but in many other tasks, such as mindreading, empathy, our appreciation of fiction, or strategy testing (2000: 122). In all these cases, in fact, we deal with representations of possible – instead of actual – states of affairs.

Nichols and Stich thus think that the right way to understand them is to consider them as a peculiar kind of mental state, characterized by certain specific causal relations with other cognitive states and mechanisms.

The addition of a PWB, however, requires the introduction of a further component to the architecture of the mind. As remarked by Nichols and Stich, in fact, once the first supposition (the initial premise) has been added to the PWB, it is necessary to combine it with some beliefs of ours, in order to enrich the fictional context and allow the pretense to continue. For example, in the tea party scenario, from the premise "We are going to have a tea party" we can infer some other information (e.g. "We will drink some tea") but, Nichols and Stich say (2000: 122-123),

> this process of inference is not going to get very far if the only thing that is in the PWB is the pretense initiating representation. [...] In order to fill out a rich and useful description of what the world would be like if the pretense-initiating representation were true, the system is going to require lots of additional information.

This information, they say, comes directly from our Belief Box. For example, from the initial premise "We are going to have a tea party" plus a belief of the kind "Tea parties usually take place around 5 pm," I can infer that our pretense is taking place at some moment in the afternoon, around 5 pm.

The problem, however, is that our pretend representations can be – and typically are – incompatible with our beliefs. The pretender believes that the cup is empty, but supposes that it has been filled with some tea; she believes that this object is a banana, but imagines that it is a telephone, and so on. So, Nichols and Stich say (2000: 123), if our inference mechanisms could access the whole set of our beliefs plus our pretend representations, they would often have to deal with some contradiction and their functioning would probably be compromised. Since our capacity for drawing inferences during pretense seems to be preserved, it is necessary to suppose, the authors say, the existence of a dedicated mechanism, one that is able to filter from the Belief Box only those contents that are compatible with the contents of our pretend mental states, thus preventing incompatible beliefs from being computed together with our pretenses (2000: 124). This mechanism, that they call the "UpDater" (cf. fig. 3), would be then capable of "avoiding the explosion of contradictions that might otherwise arise when the pretense premises and the contents of the pretender's Belief Box are combined in the PWB."

Finally, a third element is required, according to Nichols and Stich, in order to explain how the pretend scenario can be enriched independently of the initial premise and the background knowledge that can be retrieved from the Belief Box. Pretense, the authors remark (2000: 127),

> is full of choices that are not dictated by the pretense premise, or by the scripts and background knowledge that the pretender brings to the pretense episode. The fact that these choices typically get made quite effortlessly requires an explanation.

This is why the authors introduce the "Script Elaborator," a mechanism – or, more likely, a cluster of mechanisms – "whose job it is to fill in those details of a pretense that can't be inferred from the pretense premise, the (filtered) contents of the Belief Box and the pretender's knowledge of what has happened earlier on in the pretense" (2000: *ibidem*). The restaurant scenario discussed in § I.1.3 represents a typical example of this kind of embellishment operated by the Script Elaborator. A subject who pretends to be at the restaurant typically follows a standard course of action, dictated by her knowledge about restaurants: she orders first, then gets the food, then eats, and finally pays. Now, although this "script," stored in her mind, can certainly provide the general structure for this episode of pretense, a lot of details are left unspecified. For example, as we have seen, the pretender will have to decide what she will take for dinner, whether or not the food will be good, etc. The Script Elaborator fills in all these details.

To sum up, according to Nichols and Stich's account, pretend mental states are to be conceived as suppositions, that is, as states of propositional imagination which can share their contents with some beliefs of ours, but which are characterized by a peculiar functional role within the mind. As we will see in the next paragraph, however, the theoretical choices made by Nichols and Stich are not without consequences. In particular, if one understands pretend representations as a peculiar kind of mental state, it is then difficult to explain the special analogy existing between real and pretend beliefs, since this analogy seems to be precisely a similarity in their respective functional roles.

1.3. *Problems for Nichols and Stich's account*

The main problem for Nichols and Stich's theory of imagination has been pointed out in a recent paper by the philosopher Alvin Goldman (2006a).

The problem, Goldman claims, comes directly from their proposal to consider imaginings – what they call "suppositions" – as a peculiar kind of mental state, characterized by a specific functional role, distinct from those of beliefs, desires, intentions and the like. This theoretical choice, in fact, brings with it the difficulty to explain also the "special analogy" existing between the representations contained in the PWB and those contained in the Belief Box, since this analogy seems to be precisely a similarity in their functional role. In other words, if it is true on the one hand that imaginings have different effects on our behavior with respect to genuine beliefs with the same content (for example, when the child pretends that a muddy cake is a chocolate cake, it never happens that the pretend representation of the chocolate cake induces her to eat the mud), on the other hand, it is equally true that they share several functional properties with their genuine counterparts. On most occasions a pretend representation leads us to draw the same inferences and take the same decisions we would have taken if we were dealing with a genuine representation. Moreover, Goldman rightly remarks (2006a: 45) that if suppositions really differed from beliefs for their functional role, as sustained by Nichols and Stich, then they should differ from beliefs to the same extent desires do, for desires also differ from beliefs in their functional role. Since this is not the case, then, the special analogy between beliefs and suppositions remains completely unexplained. To put it another way, by conceiving imaginings as a peculiar kind of mental state, Nichols and Stich are able to explain the differences, but not the peculiar similarities that characterize suppositions and genuine beliefs sharing the same content.

The solution proposed by Nichols in response to this problem is known as the *single-code hypothesis*. According to Nichols (2004a: 131), the representations that are in the Belief Box and those in the PWB not only share the same content, but also a common code, and it is precisely this code that assures that if a "mechanisms is *activated* by the occurrent belief that *p*, it will also be activated by the occurrent pretense representation that *p*". Since this code is only shared by beliefs and suppositions, this explains why suppositions are more similar, in their functional role, to beliefs than to desires, or to other types of mental states.

The problem, however, is that Nichols has never been able to specify what this single code could consist of, precisely, and why it would be necessary to assure that genuine beliefs and suppositions be treated in the same manner by the same cognitive mechanisms. Truly enough, the idea of a single code was already present in the original formulation of Nichols and Stich's theory of pretense (2000: 125), where the authors proposed the following interpretation:

> We have suggested that the UpDater and other inference mechanisms treat the pretense representations in roughly the same way that the mechanisms treat real beliefs, but we have said little about the representational properties and the logical form of pretense representations. One possibility that we find at-

tractive is that the representations in the PWB have the *same logical form* as representations in the Belief Box, and that their representational properties are *determined in the same way*. When both of these are the case, we will say that the representations are *in the same code*.

According to Nichols and Stich, the reason why pretend and genuine representations are treated in the same way by some cognitive mechanisms was to be found in the fact that these representations share the same logical form. A representation with content "Hamlet was the Prince of Denmark," they argued (2000: 126), has the same logical form of the belief "Charles is the Prince of Wales," and this is why some mechanisms (e.g. our inference mechanisms) can compute the former exactly the same way as they compute the latter.

In subsequent papers, however, Nichols has abandoned the notion of a logical form, since he did not want to be committed to any specific conception of the logical form (2009: p.c.) He started to speak, instead, of this code as a more generic sort of *syntactical property*, leaving completely unspecified, however, what this code could consist of. As Nichols himself recognized (2004a: 131):

> it is far from clear what the code is for representations in the Belief Box, so it is not possible to be specific about the details or the nature of the putatively shared code. But the important point for present purposes can be made without giving further detail about what the code is. If pretense representations and beliefs are in the same code, then mechanisms that take input from the pretense box and from the Belief Box will treat parallel representations much the same way.

The problem, however, Goldman replies (2006a: 46), is that it is not clear why this code should be shared only by these two types of mental states – beliefs and suppositions. For example, since beliefs and desires must also somehow 'communicate' or 'interact' in the process of practical reasoning, why shouldn't they share a common code too?

More generally, the problem with the single-code hypothesis is that it turns out to be in tension with the former hypothesis sustained by Nichols and Stich, meaning that pretend and genuine representations differ in their functional role. In other words, if the distinction between imaginings and beliefs is a distinction in the functional role of the two kinds of representations, then, how can it be true that, for every mechanism that takes in input representations coming from both the Belief Box and the PWB, the representation p, coming from the latter, will be processed in exactly the same way as the representation coming from the former? (Nichols 2004a: 131).

Nichols and Stich's theory should predict just the opposite. Of course, Goldman says, it is possible that for *some* mechanisms, genuine and pretend representations are to be computed in exactly the same manner, but what are these mechanisms and why are they – and only they – sensitive to this alleged single code?

As we will see in the second part of this chapter, the problem, according to Goldman (2006a), can be solved only by rejecting the conception of imagination proposed by Nichols and Stich and by embracing, instead, a new account of the imagination, which identifies this capacity with a kind of simulative mechanism; one by means of which we would be able to reproduce several types of mental states. On this account, suppositions do not constitute a specific kind of mental state, but rather, they are conceived as the simulative counterparts of beliefs. Before entering this discussion, however, we would like to make some final remarks on the cognitive architecture discussed so far. As we will try to show, in fact, there are some ambiguities in this architecture that still wait to be solved.

1.4. *Some worries about the boxes*

Our worries about the architecture of the mind that has been proposed by Nichols and Stich, and that nowadays is largely employed within the cognitive sciences, concern, in particular, the conception of those 'boxes' which constitute the bricks by which our minds would be made up. More precisely, what we would like to stress is that these boxes have been interpreted in several – and incompatible – ways.

Nichols and Stich themselves have been quite ambiguous about their nature. If, on the one hand, they remark that these boxes are nothing but a metaphor – "the 'box' metaphor is just a notational device for distinguishing representations that have systematically different functional or computational properties" (2000: 136) – on the other hand, they sometimes speak of them as if they were something more than this: "The PWB [*Possible World Box*] is a *work space* in which our cognitive system builds and *temporarily stores* representations of one or another possible world." (2000: 122, italics mine). What the latter quotation seems to suggest is that, far from being a mere metaphor, the PWB would rather consist in a dedicated *temporary buffer*, where our suppositions are put and acted upon by our cognitive mechanisms. A confirmation, in this sense, comes from the interpretations that other authors have given of the boxes. For example, what Peter Carruthers says, while illustrating Nichols and Stich's architecture, is the following:

N&S (2003) suggest, in fact, that *two* new boxes need to be added to the standard architecture [...] One is a mechanism for generating novel suppositions [*the Script elaborator*]. The other is a working-memory system within which those suppositions get elaborated [*the Possible Worlds Box*]. (2006: 90)

Also Carruthers, then, understands the PWB as something more than a metaphor to indicate the class of all *suppositions*. It is, rather, a temporary device, a "working-memory system" where suppositions get elaborated.

The interpretation of the PWB as a temporary device, moreover, suggests that the architecture of the mind presented by Nichols and Stich is a picture of the 'mind at work', meaning a picture which concerns only our occurrent mental states. This interpretation, however, departs significantly from the original idea of the boxes ascribable to Schiffer (1981), and this has given rise to further misunderstandings. Here is, for example, what Sperber writes about the boxes:

> So, in the functional architecture of human minds too, there has to be a database such that any representation stored in that data-base is treated as a representation of an actual state of affairs, i.e. as a belief.
>
> What makes the data-base a *data*-base, or a *belief box*, to use Stephen Schiffer's phrase, is that the representations it contains, by the very fact of being so located, are freely used as premises in practical and epistemic inferences.
>
> [...] (Such permanent boxes, which each define a basic type of mental representation, should not be confused with the temporary buffers of inference engines, where a number of premises with different cognitive statuses may be brought together for joint processing.) (1997: 68-69)

On Sperber's interpretation, the Belief Box is not to be conceived as merely a notational device, nor is it a temporary buffer, containing our *occurrent* beliefs; but rather, it is a *database*, one in which beliefs are somehow stored and thus contained as *dispositional* beliefs.[7]

---

7   Representationalists usually distinguish between *dispositional* beliefs – that is, representations of the world stored somewhere in the mind – and *occurrent* beliefs – the very same representations when they are actually present to the mind and acted upon by our cognitive mechanisms. So, for example, in my mind I have plausibly stored the information that "I was born on June, the 13th, 1977", but this information is not always present to my mind: it is a *dispositional* belief. Only when explicitly asked to declare my birthday I recall this information and thus my belief is *occurrent* in my mind. Some authors also recognize the existence of a third kind of beliefs, which they call *implicit* beliefs. The reason to postulate the existence of implicit beliefs is the following: if someone now asks me whether I

The architecture of the mind proposed by Nichols and Stich thus presents some important ambiguities, as confirmed by the conflicting interpretations that have been given of it. As we will try to show in the next section (cf. esp. § 2.3), these ambiguities can create some problems when it comes to the discussion of the role played by pretend representations in contexts such as our games of make-believe. This will become clearer as soon as we consider the recreativist theories of the imagination.

2. Recreativism

The first proposal to understand imagination as a kind of simulation was advanced by Gregory Currie and Ian Ravenscroft (Currie 1995; Currie & Ravenscroft 1997). At the beginning, however, their hypothesis did not concern imagination in general, but only some forms of imagery, such as visual and motor imagery, which would have constituted, according to their account, the simulative counterparts of visual perceptions and motor plans. Later, this hypothesis has been extended to other kinds of mental states, such as beliefs and desires (cf. Currie & Ravenscroft 2002; Goldman 2006b). This has led, then, to understand the whole imagination as a simulative mechanism, one by means of which we would be able to recreate several types of mental states at will, from lower-order mental states like perceptions and motor plans to higher-order states such as beliefs, desires, hopes, and the like. In this sense, then, Currie and Ravenscroft speak of *belief-like imaginings, desire-like imaginings, vision-like imaginings*, and so on. This is also why I have labeled this position on imagination as 'recreativism'.[8]

In what follows I will start by considering Currie and Ravenscroft's initial proposal to understand some forms of imagery as instances of simulation (§ 2.1). I will discuss how this proposal has been extended to all forms

---

think there are kangaroos on Mars, I will answer negatively. Plausibly, however, this information ("On Mars there are no kangaroos") is not really stored in my mind – that is, it is not a dispositional belief of mines – but I can easily draw it from some other dispositional beliefs (e.g. "on Mars there is no life"). In this case, then, we speak of an *implicit* belief: a propositional content that, although not explicitly represented in my mind, is part of the inferences that can be drawn from the knowledge represented in my mind (cf. the entry "Belief" in the *Stanford Encyclopedia of Philosophy*).

8   Our definition echoes the title of the famous book by Currie and Ravenscroft, *Recreative minds* (2002).

of imagination, thus collapsing the two notions into each other (§ 2.2). Finally, I will discuss the kinds of problems that are peculiar to this account of our pretend mental states (§ 2.3).

2.1. *Imagery as a kind of simulation*

The proposal to understand imagery as a kind of simulation or recreative mechanism was advanced by Currie and Ravenscroft in two papers around the middle of the '90s (Currie 1995; Currie & Ravenscroft 1997). More precisely, what Currie and Ravenscroft argued is that, since visual and motor imagery both exploit those mechanisms which are normally employed, respectively, for visual perception and motion planning, and they employ these mechanisms in order to perform other tasks – that is, to imagine some visual scenes or to imagine performing some movements –, they can both be considered as cases of off-line simulation. In other words, analogously to the Decision-making system (which can be activated not only by some of our genuine beliefs and desires, but also by pretend beliefs and desires, in order to understand and predict one's behavior), also in the case of visual and motor imagery, the authors argued, we deal with cognitive mechanisms (our visual system and our motor system), which are activated by non-standard stimuli in order to perform a *function different* from the standard one.

2.1.1. *Three defining criteria*

In order to establish whether or not visual and motor imagery can count as instances of simulation, Currie and Ravenscroft (1997: 163-164) start by individuating three defining criteria of a simulation process.

(1) The first is represented by the *asymmetric counterfactual dependence* of the simulation from the target process (the process that must be simulated). For example, if we take the Practical reasoning mechanism, Currie and Ravenscroft say, the off-line activation of this mechanism (for action prediction) counts as the simulation of a decision-making process, but the converse is not true, so we would not describe a decision-making process as the simulation of action prediction.[9]

---

9   As the authors remark (cf. 1997: 163, footnote 3), the processes we are dealing with here (i.e. Decision-making and Action prediction) are individuated on the functional, and not on the physical level: "From a physical point of view," the authors say, "as described in terms of neural processes for instances, they might count as one and the same process."

As the authors notice, this criterion directly derives from a common-sense intuition: had humans never had a decision-making system, they would have been unable not only to make decisions, but also to understand and predict others' actions. Or, to put it slightly differently, we can well imagine being able to make decisions without being able to simulate another's decision-making process, but we cannot imagine being able to simulate another's decision-making without being able to make, ourselves, decisions. This kind of intuition is also confirmed by evolutionary psychology. From the evolutionary point of view, in fact, it is highly probable that we first developed a capacity for decision-making (indispensable to make decisions in a rapid way), and that this capacity was then recruited for other tasks as well, such as understanding and predicting others' actions.

(2) The second criterion consists instead of the *type-identity* of the mechanism which is employed both in the target process and its simulation (1997: 164). Again, if we take the case of the decision-making process and the prediction of others' actions, the mechanism concerned by these two tasks is one and the same, namely: the Practical reasoning system. In other words, we are dealing with two *tokens* of the same *type*, since the mechanism at work in both cases computes the same kinds of inputs (a couple of states which have the functional role of a belief and of a desire) and gives the same kind of output (a decision).

(3) Finally, simulation implies a *variation in the causal role* of the mechanism, which is employed by the simulation process. We are dealing, here, with a reformulation of the classic idea, characteristic of the simulation theories of mindreading, according to which simulation requires the employment of a mechanism which is already part of the cognitive furnishing of the subject, but which is made to run in off-line mode (it is 'disconnected' from its standard inputs and fed with some pretend states) in order to accomplish a different task (in the case of the Decision-making system, as said above, the new task consists of understanding and predicting others' actions).

Given this notion of simulation, Currie and Ravenscroft then proceed to show that imagery can be interpreted as a form of simulation.

2.1.2. *Experimental evidence*

With respect to the first criterion indicated above – namely, the counterfactual dependence of the simulation from the target process – it seems that both visual and motor imagery easily satisfy this requisite. For example, in the case of visual imagery, it seems plausible to say that we could well be able to see a flowery meadow while being unable to imagine one, whereas it is much harder to sustain that we could imagine to see a flowery meadow if we had never seen one in our life. Analogous considerations can be made about motor imagery: imagining performing a certain movement without being able to really accomplish it seems to be very difficult, whereas the inverse is much more plausible.[10]

Moreover, as prescribed by the second and the third criterion, if visual and motor imagery are to be interpreted, respectively, as the simulation of vision and the simulation of motion, then they must be generated by running some *crucial parts* off-line, respectively, of the visual and the motor system. If this is true, the authors claim, if vision and visual imagery on the one hand, and motion and motor imagery on the other hand, really exploited the same cognitive mechanism, a series of prediction should be confirmed (1997: 164).

First of all, we should expect that visual and motor imagery have many properties in common with, respectively, vision and motion. In the case of visual imagery this hypothesis is certainly verified: we not only have a phenomenological experience that vividly resembles an experience of visual perception, but we also have the performances shown in tasks which require the experimental subjects to either see or to simply imagine a visual scene. This brings us to several analogies. For example, the time it takes to scan between two points on a real map is approximately the same time it takes to perform the same task on an imaginary map. Or, to take another example, exactly as it is possible to place a boundary on the visual field (so that the subject can decide whether or not a certain object, located at a certain place, falls within this boundary), it is also possible to locate a boundary on a merely imagined visual field, and still be able to discriminate whether or not a certain object, imagined at different places, falls within this field (cf. 1997: 165).

Much the same way, also in the case of motor imagery we can discover a relevant number of analogies between the temporal and kinematic properties of actual movements on the one hand, and those of only imagined movements on the other hand (1997: 168). For example, it is well known that the duration of an imagined movement is very close to the duration of the corresponding actual movement and that these durations both depend

---

10   It is important, here, to avoid confusion between, respectively, *external* and *internal* motor imaging. Of course, I can easily *visualize myself* in the act of performing a very complicated movement (this is a case of external motor imagination), but this does not amount to imagine – *kinaesthetically* – the execution of that movement (to *imagine moving* in a certain way).

on the same factors (e.g. the difficulty of the movement performed). Moreover, even if in the case of motor imagery, the phenomenology can be less vivid, it is not totally absent. For example, subjects asked to judge whether an image of some body part was that of a left or a right hand, reported to have had the kind of kinesthetic experience that typically characterizes the actual execution of the movement required to reach, with one's own hand, the same position of the stimulus (cf. 1997: 168-169).

A second prediction is that, if visual and motor imagery share the same cognitive mechanism with, respectively, vision and motion, then we should find a series of interferences of vision and motion on their imaginative counterparts, and vice versa, since, Currie and Ravenscroft reason, the same mechanism cannot be employed to accomplish two different tasks at the same time. Also this prediction, Currie and Ravenscroft argue, is verified by a robust amount of data. In particular, they cite a case of interference in a task of visual imagery, in which the subjects were asked to form a visual image of the letter F and then to imagine tracing around this latter. Those subjects who had had the additional task to point to another letter (a Y or an N) while doing the first task performed much worse, thus showing that the performance on a task of visual imagery can be weakened by the contemporary accomplishment of a visual task (1997: 164-165). Something analogous – although this time the effect goes in the opposite direction, from an imaginative to a non-imaginative performance – can be found in the domain of motor imagery, where, as known, the simple mental rehearsal of a certain movement (its imagination) can improve our athletic performance (giving rise, for example, to a significant increase in muscular strength, cf. 1997: 171).

Moreover, if the same cognitive mechanism is employed both by vision and visual imagery, or by motion and motor imagery, then those pathologies which affect the visual and the motor system should also have consequences, respectively, on visual and motor imagery. Concerning visual imagery, Currie and Ravenscroft cite, among others, the case of some patients affected by hemispatial neglect, who were unable not only to see one side of their visual field, but also to imagine it (cf. Bisiach & Luzzatti 1978). An analogous relation between deficiencies in motor performance and motor imagery can be found in patients affected by Parkinson's disease. Currie and Ravenscroft refer, in particular, to a study by Dominey *et al.* (1995), which has shown that patients affected to the right side of their body were significantly slower in performing a finger sequencing test not only when they were asked to perform the task with the affected hand, but also when they had to simply imagine performing that task with their right hand (cf. 1997: 170ff).

Finally, and most importantly, Currie and Ravenscroft argue, brain imaging studies should confirm the existence of a substantial overlapping between the brain areas which are involved in vision and those involved in visual imagery tasks and, analogously, between those areas which are recruited for the execution of movements and those which are activated during tasks of motor imagery. Again, this prediction has also been confirmed by several experimental data (cf. 1997: 166 and 172-173).

Since all predictions have been punctually verified, Currie and Ravenscroft conclude to the truthfulness of their initial hypothesis: instances of visual and motor imagery share with their non-imaginative counterparts at least some *crucial parts* of the same mechanism, which is then recruited, on different occasion, to perform different tasks (thus varying its causal role). Visual and motor imagery can be thus considered as, respectively, the simulation of vision and motion.

As anticipated, however, Currie and Ravenscroft have not limited their recreativist account to imagery alone, but they have extended their theory also to propositional forms of imagination. Exactly as they postulate the existence of vision-like or motion-like states, they also speak of belief-like imaginings and desire-like imaginings, that is, imaginings which have the same functional role of some genuine belief or desire of ours. In the next paragraph, I will analyze in detail the application of the recreativist approach to propositional imagination, focusing, however, on a different – even if nearly equivalent – theory, that has been recently proposed by Alvin Goldman (2006a, b). The reason is that in Goldman's work it is possible to better appreciate the changes that the recreativist approach has introduced in our conception of the imagination, leading us to conceive this capacity as a *heuristics* rather than a specific type of mental state.

2.2. *Supposition-imagination* vs. *Enactment-imagination*

Alvin Goldman (2006a) discusses the kinds of mental experiences a subject typically undergoes while she is engaged in a work of fiction – that is, when she reads a book, watches a movie, attends a play at the theater, etc. This engagement, Goldman claims, necessarily implies an act of the imagination, because the consumer must be able to imagine at least that certain states of affairs – the states of affairs depicted by the fiction – have happened or are happening at the present moment. In other words, the consumer of fiction "is invited to *suppose* that such-and-such occurs, in the absence of evidence that it actually does occur and despite disbelieving (in the typical case) that it actually occurs" (2006a: 41).

While enjoying fiction, then, the subject is perfectly aware of the fact that what is happening in the fictional work is not real, but nevertheless, she supposes that it is really happening. This supposition requires, Goldman says, a minimal act of imagination and, more precisely, an act of purely conceptual imagination which lacks, in other words, any sensory aspect and whose content can be formulated in linguistic terms with a that-clause ("Imagine that *p*"). For example, while reading *Anna Karenina*, the reader is required to imagine that "Anna is married", that "she is unhappy", that "she has fallen in love with officer Vronsky", and so on. These acts of imagination are independent from all the possible mental images that the subject could form about Anna Karenina and her situation (cf. the already-mentioned distinction between imagery and imagination, § I.3.4, footnote 20). Goldman's aim, however, is to show that this kind of imagination – what he calls *Supposition-imagination* or, briefly, *S-imagination* – is not the only form of imagination involved in our appreciation of fiction; on the contrary, as we will see in a moment, S-imagination should be reinterpreted as a special application of a more general capacity, that he calls *Enactment-imagination* (*E-imagination*).

Enactment-imagination, Goldman explains, "is a matter of creating or trying to create in one's own mind a selected mental state, or at least a rough facsimile of such a state" (2006a: 42). Typical examples of E-imagination are all sensory forms of imagination, by means of which the subject reproduces or *re-enacts* in her mind perception-like states. Visual imagination can be thus understood as a capacity for reproducing vision-like states, tactile imagination as the reproduction of touch-like states, and also motor imagination can be considered as a form of E-imagination: more precisely, as the capacity to re-enact those representational states that are directed towards actions (what we usually call "motor plans"). In this sense, then, analogously to Currie and Ravenscroft, Goldman also conceives imagination – more precisely, E-imagination – as nothing but a form of *mental simulation*, a capacity for recreating in one's own mind different types of mental states. And, just like Currie and Ravenscroft, Goldman believes this kind of imagination is not confined to sensory forms of imagination, but also includes the purely conceptual forms of imagination described above – what Goldman labels Supposition-imagination:

> How is it [S-imagination] related to E-imagination? One possible approach holds that there are two distinct kinds of imagination, with no essential connection to one another. S-imagination is *sui generis*, a type of imagination different from, and irreducible to, E-imagination. A second possible approach holds that E-imagination is the fundamental kind of imagination, and that S-imagination

is simply one species of it. Which species? It is the species in which the mental state enacted is belief. (2006a: 44)

Goldman's proposal is thus to think of suppositions themselves as the product of E-imagination and, more precisely, as the product of our capacity for re-enacting beliefs. For example, when we read *Anna Karenina* and *suppose* that the heroine has committed suicide, what we do, according to Goldman, is to *enact a belief-like state* that Anna has committed suicide: that is, we *simulate* a belief with that content. "Supposing that p", he says, "is E-imagining believing that p" and, still, "we should leave room for such states as E-imagining hoping that p, E-imagining intending to A, etc." (2006a: *ibidem*).

Both Currie and Ravenscroft's recreative theory of the imagination and Goldman's theory of the Enactment-imagination can thus be interpreted as two new formulations of the ancient thesis of the unity of the imagination. On both accounts, in fact, every form of imagination – from imagery to propositional imagination – must be understood as a *simulative* activity, one by which we can recreate or re-enact in our own mind different types of mental states. As we will try to show in the following paragraph, however, this recreativist theory of the imagination also has to face some important problems when it comes to explain the different kinds of mental states – both pretend and genuine – that a subject must hold in a context of pretense.

2.3. *Problems for recreativism*

In the first part of the chapter, we analyzed problems that characterize Nichols and Stich's conception of the imagination. In particular, we observed that, since Nichols and Stich understand our imaginings as a peculiar kind of mental state, they find themselves with the problem of explaining the 'special analogy' existing between imaginings and beliefs, meaning the fact that several mechanisms treat both types of states in exactly the same way.

The recreativist account described so far presents, instead, the opposite problem. Since recreativists consider imaginings as states that can resemble their genuine counterparts not only in their content, but also in their functional role, it remains unexplained how we could distinguish them from their genuine counterparts. How can we tell that a state of ours is an imagining rather than a belief or a desire? And why not even young children mix up their genuine and pretend beliefs?

To make the problem clearer, let us start by considering what happens during a prototypical game of make-believe, as when a child pretends that a banana is a telephone. This act of pretense, one could argue, requires two distinct beliefs from the child. On the one hand, the child must imagine that the object in her hand is a telephone, so she must form a pretend belief with the content "this is a telephone." On the other hand, it is well known that children who participate in pretense play rarely confuse the real world with the pretend one. In the majority of cases, then, the child who pretends that the banana is a telephone is perfectly aware that the banana is a banana: this is shown by the fact that, if questioned about the real nature of the object and its function in everyday life, the child correctly answers that it is a fruit, that it is edible, etc. So, one could conclude, in a typical game of make-believe like pretending-banana-is-a-telephone, a child believes, at the same time, both that "that (banana) is a banana" and that "that (banana) is not a banana" (but instead a telephone).

The problem becomes clearer if we translate Goldman's position in 'boxological terms.' If pretend beliefs do not constitute a special kind of mental state, characterized by a peculiar functional role, but are rather understood as the re-enactments of beliefs, then we are forced to admit that, during the pretense play, in one and the same box (the Belief Box) we have both a genuine representation that p ("that is a banana") and a pretend representation that q ("that is a telephone", and thus, by inference $\neg p$, "that is not a banana"). But this is not acceptable (cf. Nichols & Stich 2000: 133), because contradictory contents can only be contained in different boxes (e.g. I can desire that tomorrow be a sunny day despite believing, after having heard the weather forecast, that this will not be the case), but they cannot be contained in one and the same box at the same moment (e.g. I cannot believe that tomorrow will be a sunny day and that tomorrow will be a rainy day simultaneously).

The kind of problem we are dealing with, here, is not different from the one discussed above (cf. § 1.1) – i.e. the problem that, according to Nichols and Stich, afflicted the simulationist account of pretense suggested by Gordon and Barker (1994).[11] Also on Goldman's account, in fact, pretend beliefs are nothing but the re-enactment of beliefs or belief-like imagin-

---

11   The example suggested by Nichols and Stich was the following: "When Stich pretends that there is a burglar in the basement he simultaneously believes that there is no one in the basement. (If he didn't believe that, he'd stop pretending in a big hurry. There would be more important things to do). So it would appear that on Gordon and Barker's account Stich has two representations in his belief box, one with the content *There is a burglar in the basement* and one with the content

ings, and thus, they cannot be distinguished from genuine beliefs neither because of their content nor because of their functional role. This makes it hard to explain how the pretender can hold, at the same time, contradictory beliefs, yet not mistaking genuine and pretend representations.

It is worth noting, moreover, that the problem arises not only when the subject has to deal with contradictory beliefs (as in the case above), but also when her pretend and genuine representations share the same content. The second experimental setting ideated by Leslie (1994) is a clear example of this situation. As seen (cf. § I.1.2), in consequence of having observed the experimenter first pretending to fill a cup with some tea and then turning over the cup, the child comes to entertain two different states – a belief and a belief-like imagining – with the very same content ("The cup is empty"). On the one hand, in fact, the child gains from perception a belief that "the cup is empty"; on the other hand, she has a pretend belief with the same content, deriving from the pretend behavior she has just observed. The recreationist account thus also seems to face serious problems with this example: if the child believes and, at the same time, imagines that p (that "the cup is empty"), then we should infer that the child has a certain belief (p) and simulates or re-enacts, at the same time, that very mental state. But this fact seems to be highly implausible from a cognitive point of view, since in the same box (the Belief Box) the child should have, at the same time, two identical contents (two p) and yet he should be able to keep them distinct from one another.

A possible solution to this problem could consist in assuming a position like the so-called "suspension of belief," which has been adopted, for example, to explain our emotional responses to fiction.[12] The idea is that, when we attend to a work of fiction, we are somehow able to suspend all our beliefs about reality, that is, those beliefs are not ascribable to ourselves at that moment, and so they are not in contradiction with our beliefs about the fictional story. For example, while reading *Anna Karenina*, we would be able to suspend our beliefs that Anna is only a fictional character, that she never existed, etc., so these beliefs would not contradict our beliefs about the fictional story (e.g. that Anna Karenina is suffering for love, that she has committed suicide, etc.). The same could happen in a context of pretense: while pretending that a banana is a telephone, for example, we

---

There is no one in the basement. Something must be said to explain why these patently incompatible beliefs don't lead to an inferential meltdown" (2000: 133).

12   Cf. e.g. Anderson 1996; Tan 1996, but we will come back to this question in chapter 3 (cf. § 2.4.1).

could be able to suspend our beliefs about the actual properties of the object involved in the game (our beliefs that the banana is a fruit, that it is edible, etc.), and hold true that this object possesses some other properties (e.g. that it is a telephone).

The "suspension of belief," however, has met a poor consensus among philosophers, mainly because of the implausible notion of belief it inevitably implies: is belief something that can be suspended for a while? Since the formation and revision of beliefs seem to be widely automatic and unconscious processes, independent of our will, it is not clear at all how we could decide to suspend them, even if only for a while.

A second – and, apparently, more plausible – solution could consist in adopting the account advanced by Kevin Mulligan (1999), whose theory, although analogous to Goldman's and Currie and Ravenscroft's, diverges from the latter scholars in one important aspect, that is, in the way it conceives the nature of beliefs and their relationship with their pretend counterparts.

In his paper *La varietà e l'unità dell'immaginazione* [*The variety and unity of the imagination*], Kevin Mulligan has sustained the following thesis: 50% of all types of mental states (be they propositional or not) are imaginative in nature, in the sense that "for every imaginative kind of mental state, we can individuate a non-imaginative state which corresponds to it, and vice versa" (1999: 54, transl. mine). Moreover, Mulligan suggests that simulation could constitute the subpersonal mechanism by means of which we can explain this correspondence between imaginative and non-imaginative mental states (1999: 62).

Mulligan thus seems to share with Goldman and Currie and Ravenscroft the idea that, since imagination is nothing but the simulation or re-enactment of different types of mental states, every kind of mental state possesses an imaginative counterpart. Nevertheless, there is an important aspect, which distinguishes Mulligan's position from the other recreativist theories, and this aspect concerns precisely the nature of our beliefs. Contrary to Goldman, in fact, Mulligan does not think of beliefs as mental *events*, but rather as *dispositions*, i.e. as "traces" or "mental files" stored in our mind, which can be actualized by *judgments*. Accordingly, he claims that we cannot imagine (i.e. re-enact) the former, but only the latter: in other words, while we can simulate judgments because of their nature of mental events, beliefs, amounting to certain pieces of information stored in our mind, are something that cannot be re-enacted (cf. 1999: 57).[13]

---

13   Also Mulligan, then, adopts a representationalist account of beliefs, which distinguishes between *dispositional* beliefs – i.e. representations stored somewhere in

As a consequence, while it is possible to suppose that $\neg p$ simultaneously believing that p – this is in fact the typical move of a *reductio ad absurdum* – it is not possible, at the same time, to suppose both that $\neg p$ and to judge that p; and, much the same way, while it is possible to suppose that p simultaneously believing that p, it is not possible to suppose and to judge that p at the same moment (1999: 56-57). In other words, whereas there is nothing impossible in attributing to an individual a dispositional belief with content p and an occurrent belief (a "judgment" in Mulligan's terminology) with the same or also a contradictory content[14], it seems impossible, instead, that an individual can judge that p and, at the same time, she simulates to judge that p, because this would suppose that one and the same cognitive mechanism is recruited and activated at the same time in order to do different jobs and this, again, does not seem possible (cf. e.g. what has been said regarding our visual and motor systems, § 2.1.2).

Now, one could argue, Mulligan's account can also be applied to the description of the cognitive situation of a subject involved in a pretense scenario. In pretense contexts, one could argue in fact, the pretender possesses different mental states: on the one side, she certainly has some beliefs, stored in her mind, about the actual state of affairs; on the other hand, she imagines a certain state of affairs, so she simulates a judgment with a certain content. For example, following Mulligan, one could describe the empty-cup episode by saying that the child who attends the pretense possesses two different types of states. On the one hand, she *believes* that the cup is empty: she has, *stored in her mind*, the information "the cup is empty," deriving from the perception of the actual situation. On the other hand, in consequence of having observed the pretense, she also *imagines* that the cup is empty: she *reproduces a judgment* with the content "the cup is empty." In this sense, then, by distinguishing between dispositional and occurrent beliefs, we would not be compelled to admit that in one and the same box (the Belief Box) the child is holding two identical contents, two p (or also two contradictory beliefs, p and $\neg p$, as in the banana-like-a-telephone scenario).

This solution, however, does not work. In this episode of pretense, in fact, the child is presently observing the cup, and thus, she *judges* that the cup is empty. The content "the cup is empty", in other words, is not

---

the mind – and *occurrent* beliefs – those representations when they are actually present to the mind and acted upon by our cognitive mechanisms. Mulligan simply understands occurrent beliefs as judgments.

14   There is nothing strange in saying that we can entertain occurrent beliefs that contradict other (dispositional) beliefs of ours.

simply stored in the child's mind; it is not a dispositional belief but, rather, it is *occurrent* in her mind. At the same time, in consequence of having observed the experimenter's pretense, the child *imagines to judge* that "the cup is empty", so she must simulate a judgment with the content "the cup is empty." Consequently, in this pretend scenario the child should be *judging* that *p* (that "the cup is empty") and, at the same time, she should be *imagining to judge* that *p* – a situation that, as we have already said, is impossible from the cognitive point of view. The same holds true for the banana-like-a-telephone scenario: also in this situation, in fact, the child presently sees and acts upon the banana, so the perceptual judgment "this is a banana" is certainly occurring in her mind. At the same time, however, she should simulate a judgment with content "this is a telephone": so, again, the same cognitive mechanism would be recruited to do two different jobs in the same moment, which is impossible.

Recreativist theories of imagination, then, must also face some important problems when they have to explain our mental engagement in contexts of pretense. The problem, in particular, is to explain how we can keep our pretend representations distinct from our genuine ones without getting confused, if they can share with the latter not only their content, but also their internal functional role. An appeal to our metarepresentational abilities, in this case, seems to be indispensable.

As seen, according to Goldman this metarepresentational step amounts to employing our mentalistic concepts (concepts such as 'believing,' 'desiring,' 'intending,' and the like) in order to recognize the different kinds of mental states that we are simulating. As we have seen in the previous chapter (cf. § I.3.2), however, this phase of recognition involves two different problems. The former is that it is not clear at all how we could be able to pass from the subpersonal level – the neural level at which the simulation is accomplished – to the personal level – the level at which we classify a certain state as a belief rather than, for instance, as a desire. The idea of a neural matching existing between the simulated mental state and the neural pattern which is typical of a certain type of mental state, in fact, is far from having been demonstrated, especially for higher-order mental states such as beliefs and desires. Moreover, as observed, this kind of recognition is not enough to keep our pretend representations distinct from genuine ones: if a belief-like imagining shares with its genuine counterpart the same internal functional role, then it can be recognized as a *belief kind of mental state*, but this does not mean that it is recognized as a *pretend* belief, rather than a genuine one. To put it differently: what Goldman, and also Currie and Ravenscroft, do not explain is how belief-like imagining would differ from a genuine belief, if the difference is neither in their content nor in their functional role.

Summary of the chapter

In this chapter, I have analyzed and compared two different conceptions of the imagination, that have important consequences for the way we understand the nature of our pretend mental states.

As seen, the conception of imagination proposed by Nichols and Stich (2000) is a 'thin' one, since imagination is identified with supposition, and thus with propositional imagination alone. Consequently, Nichols and Stich conceive pretend mental states as a special kind of mental states, characterized by a peculiar functional role, similar, but not identical, to that of beliefs. Accordingly, they deny the existence of different kinds of pretend representations such as pretend desires, pretend perceptions, etc.

On the contrary, the theories of imagination proposed by Goldman (2006a, b) and Currie and Ravenscroft (2002) think of imagination as a kind of recreative mechanism, one by means of which we can re-instantiate different types of mental state. They thus admit the possibility not only of belief-like imaginings, but also of desire-like imaginings, vision-like imaginings, motion-like imaginings, and so on. This conception of the imagination is a 'thick' one, and it is necessarily committed to the thesis of the unity of the imagination: propositional and sensory imagination, from this point of view, are nothing but two species of the same genus, since they share a common, recreative nature.

As I have tried to show, however, both accounts are problematic, although for different reasons. Nichols and Stich, who take pretend representations to be a peculiar type of mental state, fail to give an explanation for the 'peculiar analogy' existing between suppositions and genuine beliefs. On the other hand, the recreativist account, according to which pretend representations are nothing but reproductions of genuine mental states, sharing with them the same functional role, has serious problems at explaining how a person involved in a pretense play can entertain, at the same time, pretend and genuine beliefs with contradictory contents, or with exactly the same content, without being puzzled or confuse them. In this sense, then, the problem for this account seems to be just the opposite faced by Nichols and Stich's account, since it has to explain how a pretend belief can be distinguished and kept separate from its genuine counterpart, if the difference can be individuated neither in its content nor in its functional role. As we will show in the next chapter, however, this is not the only problem for the recreativist approach: in particular, when it comes to desires, arguing for the existence of pretend desires is all but a simple task.

III.
MOTIVATION

Why do we pretend? What are our motivations to act according to a fictional scenario, rather than according to the way the world really is? Is it a general desire to act according to our imaginings that causes our pretend behavior, or do we need some specific mental state? In particular, if our behavior in real life is motivated by a couple of genuine mental states (a belief and a desire), does this mean that in pretense we need a pair of pretend states (a pretend belief and a pretend desire)?

As we have seen (cf. § I.3.1), the notion of 'pretend desire' traces back to the simulation theory of mindreading (Goldman 1986), according to which desire-like imaginings, together with belief-like imaginings, constitute the inputs that make our practical reasoning mechanism work off-line, thus allowing us to understand and predict the behavior of a target subject. Later, some authors (cf. Velleman 2000; Currie & Ravenscroft 2002; Goldman 2006a, b) appealed to pretend desires also to explain our capacity to understand and emotionally engage with fiction. For example, it has been argued, an emotion of pity or sorrow for Desdemona's death would not be understandable if we did not make appeal to our pretend desire that Desdemona be saved. And, analogously, our resentment and rage for Iago would be unreasonable if we did not possess a pretend desire that Iago receive a punishment for what he has done (cf. Currie & Ravenscroft 2002: 20ff.).

In this chapter, I will start by reviewing the arguments that have been given in favor of and against the need to admit the existence of pretend desires and I will conclude that pretend desires are not *necessary* in order to explain pretense. My aim, however, will not be confined to discuss the necessity of admitting pretend desires, but I will instead also take into consideration a more fundamental question that has still not been posed, namely, are pretend desires really *possible*? In the second part of the chapter I will thus try to show that, given a certain concept of what a desire is (ascribable to Peter Carruthers 2006), it is impossible to trace a distinction between genuine and pretend desires. I will conclude that philosophers such as Currie and Ravenscroft and Goldman should either drop the notion of 'pretend desire' or specify a notion of desire that allows them to distinguish our genuine desires from the desires we entertain regarding fictional scenarios.

1. *Are pretend desires really necessary?*

1.1. *Pretense and motivation*

In the debate concerning the existence of pretend desires we can basically distinguish two opposing positions. The first traces back to the Humean Theory of Motivation (from now on, HTM), according to which our intentional actions – thereby including our pretend actions – must be causally explained by appealing to a pair of genuine states: a belief and a desire. Among the most outstanding current supporters of the Humean Theory are Nichols and Stich, according to whom the pretender's actions are motivated by *a genuine desire to pretend in accordance to a certain fictional scenario* (that is, in accordance to some representations stored in the Possible Worlds Box)[1]:

> the pretender engages in the pretense action because she wants to behave in a way similar to the way some person or object would behave in a possible world scenario. (2003: 38)

On the contrary, as seen above, recreativism introduced the idea that, by means of the imagination, we can reproduce not only belief-like states but also other types of mental states, including desire-like states. The latter, when combined with some belief-like imagining, can motivate our behavior in exactly the same way genuine beliefs and desires do. By a recreativist account, then, pretense constitutes a counterexample to the

---

1   To be sure, there is no such thing as one 'Humean account of pretense', as Humeans themselves can disagree about the contents of the beliefs and desires involved in the pretend behavior. In a recent paper, Eric Funkhouser and Shannon Spaulding (2009) distinguished at least two Humean accounts of motivation: a broader and a narrower one. The broader account implies the acceptance of what they call the 'Belief-Desire Thesis,' according to which, "for every intentional action, there is a belief-desire pair that both causes and rationalizes that intentional action." The narrower account implies the acceptance of the additional 'Motivation-as-Desire Thesis,' according to which, "desire, and only desire, is the motivation behind every action" (cf. 2009: 292). In this sense, Nichols and Stich's account is a narrow one, since it supposes that our actions in pretense are specifically motivated by the desire to pretend in accordance to the contents of our imaginings.

standard HTM, since we are dealing with behaviors motivated by states that are not genuine beliefs and desires of ours.

In what follows, we will proceed by first considering the main objections that have been raised against the Humean account of pretense (§ 1.2), as well as the replies that can be made to these objections (§ 1.3). Then, we will consider the positive arguments formulated by Currie and Ravenscroft (2002) and Velleman (2000) in favor of the existence of desire-like imaginings (§ 1.4), which will be followed by a discussion of their possible flaws (§ 1.5).

1.2. *Against the Humean account of pretense*

In a recent paper, Funkhouser and Spaulding (2009) identified at least four main objections to the HTM.

(1) According to the first, if we stand by a Humean account of pretense, we are compelled to admit that very young children also possess the concept of pretense. If, as sustained by Nichols and Stich (2003: 38), the child is motivated to act by a genuine desire *to pretend* in accordance to what she is imagining, then the notion of pretense is part of the content of her desire. But, Currie and Ravenscroft argue (2002: 127, 213-214), it is quite implausible that 2-year-olds possess the concept of pretense, at least as a full-blown concept as that possessed by adults. In this sense, then, the Humean account would have the unwelcome consequence of 'over-intellectualizing' the pretense behavior. This problem has also been recognized by David Velleman (2000: 157), who formulated two additional objections.

(2) The former is that the Humean account would leave the child outside the pretense: if pretense were motivated by a desire about the pretense itself (the desire *to pretend* in accordance to a certain imaginary scenario), then, Velleman claims, the child would live outside the pretense. Velleman appeals here to the already-mentioned distinction between *acting for the sake of* something and *acting out of* something[2] (cf. § I.2.2), and observes:

> the child can be said to enter into the imaginary world only if the child acts *out of* her imagining, that is, only if she is motivated from within the point-of-view that she is imagining. Thus, only if Stacey [a girl involved in a game of make-believe, A/N] is motivated by her 'beliefs' and 'desires' within the fiction, is she acting *out of* the perspective of the character she is pretending to be (and not merely out of a desire to behaviorally represent it) and *really* entering into the fiction. (Funkhouser & Spaulding 2009: 296)

---

2   Although he uses different terminology (cf. 2000: 257).

(3) Moreover, Velleman claims, the Humean account denies the creativity of children's pretense. According to the HTM sustained by Nichols and Stich, a child who wants to pretend to be an elephant is motivated by the desire to act like an elephant (that is, in accordance to the imagined scenario "being an elephant"), and thus she will behave according to her knowledge of how elephants behave. But, Velleman objects, pretense often contradicts our knowledge of the real world. For example, as we have already seen in § I.1.3, while acting out a fancy-restaurant scenario, the person who pretends to be the waiter can decide to bring to his customer a Japanese sword instead of a standard meat knife, thus departing significantly from what would happen in an analogous real situation. In exactly the same way, a child can decide to pretend to be an elephant by adopting a behavior that contradicts her knowledge about how elephants actually behave (for example, she can pretend that the elephant is capable of speaking with other elephants). In Velleman's view, the Humean account cannot give an explanation for cases like this.

(4) Finally, Currie and Ravenscroft (2002) especially insisted on the fact that the Humean account of pretense is not able to satisfactorily explain our attitudes – and particularly our emotions – toward fictional situations and characters. However, since this point is not only an argument against the HTM, but it is employed to argue in favor of the existence of desire-like imaginings, we will postpone discussing it to § 1.4 in this chapter.

Before considering the reasons that have been provided in favor of the existence of pretend desires, however, let us first consider the replies to these objections.

1.3. *Defending the Humean account*

In their paper on motivation and pretense, Funkhouser and Spaulding convincingly replied to the objections raised against the Humean view by Vellman (2000) and Currie and Ravenscroft (2002). More precisely:

(1) With respect to the first objection – the necessity to ascribe the concept of pretense to young children as well – the authors object that the Humean account is committed, at most, to sustain that children possess a *behavioral* understanding of pretense, but not a *mentalistic* one. In other words, what children desire is not *to pretend that p*, but rather *to behave as if p* were the case. As the authors say:

> the child's desire to pretend is simply a desire to behave in a certain way, and
> the child's beliefs about pretending, therefore, are simply beliefs about what

sort of behavior would satisfy his desire. That the child has a desire to behave in a way that is in fact pretending does not entail that the child has conceptual knowledge of pretense. [...] The Humean is only committed to the child possessing a motivation to act in a way that as a matter of fact counts as pretense. The child need not recognize that action as pretense, however. (2009: 300)

(2) With respect to the second objection, according to which only by the "Imagination-as-Motivation" account is the pretender fully situated and absorbed in the imaginary world, Funkhouser and Spaulding reply by stressing the importance of always being 'detached' – at least to some extent – from the pretense. If Velleman finds the idea that children can pretend exactly like adults (meaning that they can be completely aware of the fictionality of the pretend scenario) to be depressing, for Funkhouser and Spaulding this is a very comforting fact, since, they argue, if children were completely absorbed, then they would be simply deluded subjects (2009: 301-302).

(3) Moreover, Funkhouser and Spaulding argue, by the Humean account, pretenders need not renounce their creativity. The picture of the Humean view sketched by Velleman with regard to this point, the authors say, is not fair. More precisely, all the Humean account requires from pretenders is that they have "a genuine desire to act out their imaginings," but it puts no constraints on the contents of these imaginative states (2009: 302). Therefore, it does not require that pretenders act in accordance with their knowledge of the real world nor does it require that their pretense mirrors reality in all respects.

(4) Finally, with respect to the fourth objection, Funkhouser and Spaulding claim that "The Humean and Anti-Humean are on par with problems concerning attitudes toward fictional narratives and attitudes toward fictional characters and situations" (2009: 302). Let us consider this last point, then, in more detail.

1.4. *In favor of desire-like imaginings*

As anticipated (cf. §§ I.3.1-I.3.2) in the recreativist account endorsed by Currie and Ravenscroft (2002) and Goldman (2006a, b), the existence of pretend desires or desire-like imaginings is indispensable, first of all, in mindreading. In order to make our Practical reasoning system work off-line, we need to feed it not only with a pretend belief, but also with a pretend desire. Appealing to one of our real desires, Currie and Ravenscroft stress, would not be enough, since in simulation we often have to imagine desiring something we do not really want: "Projection can involve more than just a shift of belief; sometimes I need to shift my desires as well, because in the imagined situation I would desire something I don't actually desire." Moreover, since genuine desires "have connections to actions, if imagining led me to have desire appropriate to a merely imagined situation, I might end up acting inappropriately." Currie and Ravenscroft thus conclude that "[t]he shift of desire must itself be a shift in imagination. There must be desire-like imaginings, as well as belief-like imaginings" (2002: 20).

In this sense, Nichols remarked (2004b: 330), the need to presuppose the existence of desire-like imaginings is compelling only for a simulationist account: if one does not believe that we need to simulate others' mental states in order to understand their behavior, there is no need to postulate the existence of pretend desires. Currie and Ravenscroft, however, have provided two further reasons in favor of the existence of pretend desires.

The first is that "postulating desire-like imaginings helps explain the affective consequences of imagination" (2002: 20). A great number of emotions – in particular, those which are called "secondary" or "cognitive" emotions – are supposed to be generated, Currie and Ravenscroft observe, not only by certain epistemic states, but also by appropriate conative states. For instance, in order to feel an emotion of envy, one must possess not only the belief that someone else has something desirable, but also the desire to have the same kind of thing. Believing that my friend John has obtained a good job, while I am still unemployed, does not make me feel automatically envious – it could well be the case that I am just a very lazy person and I have no desire at all to get a job. In order to feel envy towards my friend, I must possess not only the appropriate belief (the belief that John possesses a desirable job), but also the appropriate desire (the desire to get the same kind of job myself). The same is also true, Currie and Ravenscroft observe, for our emotional reactions to fiction: in at least some cases, the affect produced by a certain fictional scenario seems to be justifiable only by appealing to pretend desires, in addition to our pretend beliefs. An example is represented by the different emotional reactions that we have towards Desdemona's and Macbeth's deaths, respectively. In the case of Desdemona, we have a belief-like imagining that her death is the consequence of a wicked design, and thus we have also a desire-like imagining that Desdemona be saved and Iago punished. This is why we feel pity for her and we are so sad when she dies. On the contrary, in the case of Macbeth we *want* him to suffer because of what he has done, and so, again, we have not only a belief-like imagining that Macbeth is a bad person, but also a desire-like imagining about what should happen to him, and both contribute to generate certain emotional reactions (e.g. anger or resentment) towards this character.

Moreover, Currie and Ravenscroft argue, admitting the existence of desire-like imaginings can help explain some apparent contradictions in our desires. For example, as said, while watching *Othello*, we typically entertain the desire that Desdemona be rescued; at the same time, however, we do not want *Othello* to have a happy ending: on the contrary, we are glad that it ends tragically. Now, Currie and Ravenscroft observe, if these were both genuine desires of ours, we would end up with maintaining an unreasonable position, desiring both that *p* (that Desdemona is saved) and that *not p* (that Desdemona dies) at the same time. According to the authors, the solution consists in once again recognizing the existence of desire-like imaginings:

> Part of the inner tension one experiences on watching the play derives from the fact that we experience a desire-like imagining that Desdemona flourish, combined with a (genuine) desire that the play be one which will ensure that that desire-like imagining is unsatisfied. In that case, desire-like imaginings do not seem dispensable, even in those contexts where dispensing with them seems most likely to work, namely where there is an independently acknowledged fiction to appeal to. (2002: 21-22)

The reason why desire-like imaginings are indispensable in this case is that they are not subjected to the same constraints that characterize our genuine desires. "Desires," Currie and Ravenscroft say, "like beliefs, face normative constraints," but "the constraints on real desire do not govern what we call 'wanting Desdemona to be saved'" (2002: *ibidem*). So, if we cannot hold at the same time two desires with contradictory contents, we can well hold a genuine desire and a desire-like imagining with incompatible contents.

1.5. *Against desire-like imaginings*

In his review of *Recreating Minds*, Nichols (2004b) took into consideration and criticized in detail the arguments presented by Currie and Ravenscroft in favor of the existence of desire-like imaginings, paying special attention to the alleged necessity to admit pretend desires in order to explain our emotional reactions to fiction.

First, Nichols observes (2004b: 331), the range of emotions which require not only a pretend belief but also a pretend desire for their existence seems to be very limited. For example, he says, I can easily imagine that my spouse has been unfaithful and, as a consequence, I feel jealous. This probably happens because the depiction of this imaginary scenario (a belief-like imagining that "my spouse has been unfaithful") is accompanied by certain genuine desires that I have about my spouse (2004b: *ibidem*). When it comes to fiction, however, a case like this is much harder to find:

> I cannot easily generate jealousy-affect by imagining that Anna Karenina is unfaithful. One explanation for this is just that I don't have the relevant real desires when it comes to Anna. I can, of course, try to figure out how Alexey Karenin feels by imagining how I would feel were my spouse to be unfaithful. But this need not involve any desire-like imagining. As a result, even though there are emotions that plausibly do depend on desires, it is not clear that these emotions are ever generated by desire-like imaginings. (2004b: 331-332)

In the case of fiction, Nichols thus seems to suggest, I do not need to recreate any desire-like imagining in order to understand and appreciate the work. Rather, I can simply bring forth some of my genuine desires by imagining a situation which is analogous to the one depicted in the fiction.

Coming to the thesis according to which, if we did not admit pretend desires, we would end up with contradictory (genuine) desires, Nichols observes that this thesis relies on an "unargued presupposition," meaning that the fact of entertaining contradictory desires must be necessarily unreasonable or somehow problematic for the subject (2004b: 332). As we have seen, according to Currie and Ravenscroft, it is possible to desire both that *p* and that *not p* only if one is a genuine desire and the other a desire-like imagining. Even in this case, however, the authors say that we cannot avoid feeling some tension (cf. the quotation above, § 1.4) provoked by the conflicting contents of our states. But, Nichols replies, why should we experience a tension when we have two contradictory desires? Moreover, why should this tension be provoked by a conflict between a real and a pretend desire, rather than by two real desires? There is no reason, in principle, Nichols claims, to suppose that we cannot hold two genuine but conflicting desires:

> One desire is that the fiction have it that Desdemona be saved; the other desire is that the play be tragic. I both want it to be the case (fictionally, of course) that Othello not kill Desdemona, and I also want it to be the case that the narrative be tragic. (2004b: *ibidem*)

Currie and Ravenscroft, however, seem to anticipate this kind of objection when they observe:

One problem with the proposal is that it obscures the distinction between attitudes towards characters, like Desdemona, and attitudes towards fictions, like *Othello*. On the proposal, everything that has the appearance of being a desire-like state concerning fictional characters turns out to be a real desire concerning the fictional narratives that describe them. (2002: 21)

Claiming, as Nichols does, that the theatergoer does not have a pretend desire that Desdemona not be murdered, but rather a real desire that, *in the fiction*, Desdemona not be murdered amounts to claiming, according to Currie and Ravenscroft, that the theatergoer has a real desire concerning the fiction, rather than a desire-like imagining concerning the character itself. "[E]verything that has the appearance of being a desire-like state concerning fictional characters turns out to be a real desire concerning the fictional narratives that describe them" (2002: *ibidem*). But, Currie and Ravenscroft object, just as desiring that *p* (that "Desdemona not be murdered") is different from desiring that "possibly *p*" (where "possibly" stands for a modal operator), it is also different from desiring that "fictionally *p*" (that "in the fiction Desdemona not be murdered").

As we will show in the next section, Nichols and Stich's account – at least in its 'amended' version, proposed by Carruthers (2006) – is not committed to accept these desires, desires that are about the fiction and not about the characters themselves. Before discussing this point, however, we want to consider one last and, in our view, fatal objection that has been raised by Funkhouser and Spaulding (2009) against the idea of desire-like imaginings. The case concerning our emotions and desires towards fictional characters such as Desdemona is, again, a good example with which to illustrate the kind of problem that the authors have pointed out.

As we have seen, according to Currie and Ravenscroft's account, although we feel sorrow for Desdemona's death and have a desire-like imagining that she be saved, this desire does not motivate us to act: "A theatergoer who has the prescribed desire-like imagining that Desdemona be saved has no motivation to actually save Desdemona. [...] This theatergoer's imagining does not motivate *because* it is merely imaginary!" (2009: 303). But, if things were so, Funkhouser and Spaulding object, then we would get a "fragmented picture" of the imagination because some desire-like imaginings would have a motivating power – typically desire-like imaginings in contexts of pretense – whereas others – such as our desires towards fiction – would not. As a consequence, motivation, which is typically conceived as an essential feature of desires, would become a mere accidental property, something that desire-like imaginings can possess but is not intrinsic to their nature.

Moreover, the authors remark, when Currie and Ravenscroft come to consider this problem and try to offer an explanation for the different motivating powers of our pretend desires, they appeal to a kind of holism of the mind which, in the end, goes exactly against their original theory:

> So while the passive daydreamer and the active war game player may not differ in their imaginings, they will differ in their relevant mental backgrounds: the game player really desires to play a game, really believes that she is playing a game, and the passive imaginer does not have that belief or that desire. (2002: 118)

As Funkhouser and Spaulding rightly object, however, this answer is an admission, even if unintentional, that pretense is motivated not only by pretend desires, but also by some *genuine* background beliefs and desires of the agent (2009: 304).

To sum up, if on the one hand Nichols has shown that those cases to which recreativists usually appeal, in order to argue for the necessity of desire-like imaginings, can be satisfactorily explained by appealing to genuine desires of ours, on the other hand Funkhouser and Spaulding have provided an argument against the existence of desire-like imaginings. More precisely, what they have shown is that if one admits the existence of desire-like imaginings, one must give up the general principle that "the motivational powers of a mental state type are intrinsic to typical members of that type," since, as we have seen, not all desire-like imaginings seem to be able, *ceteris paribus*, to motivate our behavior.

2. *Are pretend desires really possible?*

As hinted at the beginning of this chapter, the debate concerning pretend desires has always focused on the need to admit their existence in order to explain certain cognitive activities of ours, and so far we have analyzed in detail the arguments that have been proposed in favor or against this necessity. Still, both proponents and opponents of pretend desires or desire-like imaginings have never put into question *whether the notion of a pretend desire really makes sense in itself*. In other words, the discussion about pretend desires has never been accompanied by a more general reflection about the nature of desires themselves, and the authors who have been considered so far have never specified which conception of desire they endorse. As I will try to show, however, depending on the notion of desire adopted, it does not immediately follow that desires can be simulated, and thus, that we can speak of 'pretend desires'.

In this section, I will start by considering the theory of motivation that I favor, the one proposed by Carruthers, which seems very close to a pleasure-based theory of desire. I will try to show that, in this kind of theory, the notion of a desire-like imagining does not make any sense: given this theory of desire, in fact, it is impossible to make a distinction between a genuine and a pretend desire.

This section will develop in the following manner. In § 2.1 I will start by considering the criticisms that Carruthers (2006) has aimed at Nichols and Stich's theory of motivation, and in §§ 2.2-2.3 I will illustrate how Carruthers has tried to solve these problems by combining Nichols and Stich's architecture of the mind with Damasio's theory of somatic markers, thus embracing a pleasure-based theory of desire. In such a theory, in order to argue for the existence of pretend desires, one should argue in favor of the existence of pretend emotions; but, as I will try to show, there is no possibility for discriminating between genuine and pretend emotions (§ 2.4) – at least in the case of basic emotional reactions as those that are involved in desire. As a consequence, I will argue that there is no possibility for distinguishing genuine from pretend desires (§ 2.5).

2.1. *Problems with Nichols and Stich's theory of motivation*

Peter Carruthers has recently proposed a convincing account of how pretense can be motivated that he himself labeled a "hybrid theory," since it combines the cognitive architecture of the mind designed by Nichols and Stich (2000) with the theory of somatic markers developed by Damasio (1994). More precisely, the need to 'correct' Nichols and Stich's architecture with the hypothesis of somatic markers derives, according to Carruthers, from the fact that their theory of motivation encounters some important problems.

The first problem consists in that if we adopt Nichols and Stich's theory, then we are compelled to sustain that *every* supposition whatsoever gives rise to a desire to behave as if the supposition were true. Their theory of motivation, Carruthers remarks, in fact implies the existence of a direct link between the PWB and the Desire Box such that "whenever a novel supposition is generated, [...] this causes a novel desire to come into existence: the desire, namely, to behave as one would behave if the supposition were true" (2006: 92).

The problem, however, is that the Script Elaborator (the mechanism responsible for the production of our suppositions) and the PWB (the place were these suppositions are temporarily stored) are both employed not only in pretense, but for other tasks as well, such as hypothetical and counterfactual reasoning.[3] Consequently, if every supposition in our PWB were able to generate a desire to behave according to that supposition, we should be motivated to act not only in contexts of pretense, but also when we simply entertain some hypotheses and reason about them. Since this is not the case, Carruthers says, Nichols and Stich must explain why this happens only in pretense (2006: *ibidem*).

Perhaps, Carruthers suggests, the generation of a desire to pretend according to one's own suppositions could depend on a more general, pre-existing desire to pretend *something*, but this hypothesis is admittedly highly implausible. On the contrary, we often have the impression that it is the depiction of a certain imaginary situation which is responsible for the generation of the desire to act in accordance to it. For example, Carruthers says, while remarking the resemblance between a banana and a telephone, the child could acquire a desire to pretend to make a telephone call (cf. 2006: 93-94).

Moreover, a general desire to pretend something does not explain why we decide to act according to some suppositions rather than others. That is, why "people pretend to be, or to do, things that they find in some way admirable or valuable," whereas they tend to avoid pretending according to unconformable scenarios. For example, children who admire soldiers are typically inclined to play war games, whereas children who admire homemakers usually pretend to take care of a baby, to cook a pie, and so on. True enough, Carruthers goes on, children can pretend to be or to do almost anything. For example, they can pretend to eat a meal they hate, or they can pretend to be a dead cat, but it is a matter of fact that

> children don't often engage in these forms of pretence. And when they do, their pretence can plausibly be explained as being instrumentally, rather than intrinsically, motivated. Children who engage in forms of cooperative role-play (such as doctors and patients) may have to take their turn at playing the less desirable role, for example. And children can engage in strange and unexpected forms of play in order to make other people laugh. (2006: *ibidem*)

A general desire to pretend in accordance to our suppositions, then, cannot explain our greater or lesser willingness to engage in a certain game of make-believe.

---

3   For example, someone could ask me: "Suppose that we are at a party and a friend accidentally spills some wine on your shirt. How would you react?". In this case, I have to depict an imaginary situation, as in a game of make-believe, but my purpose is simply that of predicting my reaction, not to behave accordingly.

Finally, Carruthers claims, Nichols and Stich face a problem in explaining why uses of the imagination other than pretense can involve some form of motivation. According to Nichols and Stich's account, in fact, whereas the apparatus constituted by the PWB, the Script Elaborator and the Up-Dater is shared by all forms of imagination, such as those involved in fantasy, novel-reading, counterfactual thinking, etc., what seems distinctive of pretense is the fact that it also involves our motivational systems. The representations stored in the PWB create a genuine desire in us to act in accordance with them, thus giving rise to certain behaviors. But all the activities listed above, Carruthers remarks, also seem to require the activation of our motivational systems, at least when they raise some emotional reactions. For example,

> imagined sex can make you sexually aroused, imagined insults and slights can make you angry, imagined dangers can make you afraid, and so on. Similarly, people experience a whole range of emotions when reading carefully crafted novels, and often have desires regarding the fates of the characters therein. And likewise, when I mentally rehearse what might happen when I go to see my boss to demand a raise, the result can bring me out in a cold sweat. All of this suggests very strongly that there ought to be an arrow direct from the possible worlds box to the systems that generate desires and emotions. (2006: 96)

In other words, even if not all forms of imagination give rise to an overt behavior, this does not mean that the involvement of the motivational systems is a peculiarity of pretense alone, as Nichols and Stich would instead seem to maintain. As said above, all these problems can be satisfactorily explained, Carruthers claims, if one corrects Nichols and Stich's architecture of the mind with Damasio's theory of somatic markers. Let us consider Damasio's proposal, then, in more detail.

2.2. *The theory of somatic markers*

In his famous book *Descartes' Error* (1994: cf. esp. pp. 214ff), Damasio presented a hypothesis concerning the role that our emotions play in practical reasoning, compelling us to rethink, in particular, our notion of practical rationality. This hypothesis relies on the studies conducted by the neuroscientist on a number of patients who presented bilateral damage to their ventromedial prefrontal cortices.

Damasio's patients showed problematic behavior, facing great difficulties in everyday life. When asked which steps are necessary to carry out a certain action, they had no problems and could list in the right sequence all actions one must perform in order to obtain a certain goal, but when they had to proceed from the theoretical planning to its practical implementation, they were unable to realize their plans, often acting in an erratic and counterproductive way. At the same time, they also showed problems at the emotional level, being capable of saying which emotion a certain scenario should induce, but incapable of feeling it by themselves. For example, they could tell whether and why a certain picture was disturbing, but they themselves could not feel any distress when looking at the image.

While studying these patients, Damasio came to the conclusion that the two problems had to be related. In order to test his hypothesis, his research team created an experiment that simulated real-life decision-making.[4] In brief, experimental subjects were given a certain amount of money and were faced with four decks of cards. Their goal was to gain as much as possible by sampling cards from the four decks, but whereas some cards were rewarding, others carried a penalty. More precisely, decks A and B contained cards which gave higher earnings but even higher penalties, while decks C and D gave lower gains but even lower penalties, so that, by sampling cards mainly from these latter decks, the subject could win, whereas by sampling cards mainly from the former, she was destined to lose.

The subjects, however, were not aware of the difference exiting between the decks, nor they could infer this difference by means of a simple calculation. Rather, after having played for a while, normal subjects developed a kind of 'intuition' about the badness or goodness of the decks. That is, after encountering a few losses, they typically began to choose cards mainly from decks C and D, while avoiding decks A and B. The same, however, did not happen in the case of the patients with damage to the prefrontal lobes, who continued to choose randomly, thus loosing their money.

The interesting point is that Damasio and his colleagues succeeded in correlating this difference with a difference in the unconscious emotional reactions of normal people *vs.* neurological patients. More precisely, whereas normal subjects, after a few losses, began to generate a skin conductance response before selecting a card from the 'bad' decks, the neurological patients had no emotional reaction towards them. These results thus led Damasio to formulate his famous "somatic-markers hypothesis."

According to this hypothesis, when we undergo a certain experience which raises in us a relevant emotional reaction, our experience is 'marked' by the emotion itself, so that, when we are faced with an analogous scenario, the same emotion arises. For example, in the experimental scenario

---

4   For details cf. Bechara *et al.* (1994).

described above, the experience of sampling a card from deck A or B is marked by a negative emotion because of the high losses it provokes. As a consequence, when normal subjects were thinking about the possibility of taking a card from one of the 'bad' decks, the scenario envisaged again produced this negative emotion, thus inducing them – although unconsciously – to reconsider and choose a card from the 'good' decks. On the contrary, the patients with frontal damage, who lacked this negative emotional response, could not rely on this unconscious cue and thus tended to choose cards from the decks with the highest earnings (but also the highest penalties), ultimately losing their money.

2.3. *A hybrid account*

According to Damasio, when we reason about what to do, we can envisage different scenarios, each depicting a different action to perform. For example, the subject can first imagine taking a card from deck A (one of the 'bad decks'). As said, however, acting out this scenario is marked by a negative emotion, since when the subject chose a card from this deck, she lost a large amount of money. This means, in 'boxological terms,' that the supposition "taking a card from A" is received as input by the Emotion-Formation System, which responds to it by producing a series of changes – both neural and physical – which are distinctive of a certain negative emotion. These changes, in turn, are monitored by the somatosensory system, with the consequence that the action at stake is marked as 'less desirable' and thus has no (or poor) motivational power. On the contrary, if the subject imagines taking a card from one of the 'good' decks, this supposition probably produces a positive emotion, thus acquiring higher motivational power. Now the same holds, according to Carruthers, for every supposition whatsoever:

> When we are reasoning about what to do, the various actions open to us are entertained as suppositions and entered into the possible worlds box. [...] All of these contents [...] are made available as inputs to the desire-generating and emotion-generating mechanisms. The latter set to work processing that input and produce a suite of emotional/bodily reactions. These are monitored, and our motivations towards executing the envisaged actions are adjusted up or down as a result, depending upon the valence (positive or negative) of the emotions in question. (2006: 102)

Take, for example, the supposition "that [banana] is a telephone," contained in the PWB. From this supposition, Carruthers says (2006: 104), the child could easily conclude, by means of her inferential mechanisms, that

"that [banana] can be used to call Grandma." The mental rehearsal of the action of calling Grandma, together with the depiction of its direct consequences (e.g. the possibility of having a conversation with Grandma), are received as input by the child's motivational systems. If we suppose that she loves her grandma, and also loves talking with her, then she will certainly experience a positive emotion as a result. This positive emotion, Carruthers says, will then be noted by the somatosensory monitoring system, which will mark the envisaged action as a desirable one:

> The child mentally rehearses the action schema, experiences a positive emotion, and thereby comes to desire the execution of that action schema. So her goal, when she acts, is *to talk to Grandma on that* [banana]. (2006: 106)

By combining Damasio's theory of somatic markers with the architecture of the mind designed by Nichols and Stich, Carruthers is then able to explain all the problems that afflicted Nichols and Stich's account of motivation (cf. § 2.1). First of all, he can easily explain why not all suppositions give rise to a desire to act in accordance to them; since the production of a desire depends on the emotions raised by a certain possible scenario, only those scenarios which cause a positive reaction are marked as desirable and thus actually motivate our behavior.

This, in turn, explains why we are not prone to pretend every scenario whatsoever and why there can be great individual differences: a tea-party scenario can produce a highly positive emotional reaction in one child and a negative reaction in another child, depending on their preferences and their previous experiences with that scenario.

Finally, according to this account, every use of the imagination – not only the suppositions employed in pretense, but also, for example, the scenarios we imagine when we read or watch fictional works – can have an influence on our motivational systems. Let us consider Desdemona's example again: by relying on Carruthers' theory, we can imagine the following story. When the theatergoer attends *Othello*, she envisages that Desdemona is about to die and, since she is sympathetic with Desdemona, she will probably react with an emotion of sorrow, marking this scenario as undesirable. The depiction of the alternative scenario ("Desdemona survives"), on the contrary, will probably produce a positive reaction. At the same time, however, the theatergoer will easily understand that, should the story have a happy ending, the spirit of the work would be completely distorted, and these thoughts, in turn, will also cause her a negative emotion that will motivate her to prefer the former scenario. By this account, then, we can conclude that the tension (cf. § 1.4) arises from the consecutive depiction of two different scenarios: the former is the depiction of Desdemona surviving, which is marked by a positive emotion, the latter is the depiction of the consequences of this scenario (the fact that the story will have a happy ending and thus distort the spirit of the work), which instead produces a negative emotion. As a consequence, the idea that Desdemona survives becomes undesirable too, because it is the cause of such a nauseatingly happy ending.

As it was for Nichols and Stich, then, also by Carruthers's account what the theatergoer desires is not that "in the *fiction* Desdemona be saved," but she simply possesses a representation with content "Desdemona is saved" that will probably be marked as desirable in the first place, and then will become undesirable because of the undesirable consequences to which it leads. Moreover, as just seen, by adopting the revised version of Nichols and Stich's account we are also able to explain the tension characterizing cases like this without appealing to desire-like imaginings. Rather, the tension is created by the fact that the representation at stake ("Desdemona is saved") is marked by a positive emotion – and thus it is a *genuine* desire – but its consequences result undesirable, and thus the subject can conclude that this scenario is not really worth obtaining.

2.4. *Recreating emotions*

As we have seen, Carruthers conceives of desires as occurrent mental states that represent certain non-actual scenarios and that cause in us a certain degree of pleasure which, in turn, possesses motivating power, thus making us prone to realize the scenario represented. Now, given this conception of desire as a composite state – a state which has not only a representational content, but also an emotional and motivational aspect – one could ask whether and in what sense can we distinguish genuine from pretend desires. More precisely, it could be claimed that pretend desires differ from genuine desires in at least one of these two aspects.

The first, however, does not seem to be a good candidate. The desires we entertain during an episode of pretense have the same representational content as the desires we entertain in real life: desiring to have an ice-cream for real is not different from desiring to have an ice-cream in a game of make-believe, since in both cases what we represent is a state-of-affairs that is *not actual*, but only hypothetical.[5] In other words, even during pretense, we en-

---

5   Of course, one could object that when I depict a future scenario such as "eating ice-cream," this 'concrete' possibility is not the same as the implausible scenario

visage a certain *possible* – that is, *non-actual* – scenario, and this act of the imagination has certain effects on our emotional and motivational systems. It could be argued, then, that pretend desires differ from genuine desires in their *emotional component*, that is, in the kind of pleasure or displeasure they produce. In this case, arguing in favor of the existence of pretend desires would amount to arguing in favor of the existence of pretend emotions. So the question is: are the emotions raised by the depiction of a certain possible scenario really different from the emotions raised by an actual scenario? And consequently, can we really draw a distinction between genuine and pretend emotions?

This problem has been widely explored in the domain of aesthetics and, more precisely, within the famous debate concerning the so-called "paradox of fictional emotions." Discussing whether our emotional responses towards fictional scenarios should be considered as pretend rather than genuine emotions, in fact, is tantamount to asking what the conditions for idevidiating a genuine emotion are and in what way, exactly, a pretend emotion would differ from a genuine one.

In what follows, we will briefly recapitulate the discussion about the paradox of fictional emotions, paying particular attention to the influential position held by Walton, according to whom our emotional reactions towards fiction cannot be considered as genuine ones, but rather as *quasi-emotions*. As we will try to show, however, this position seems to contrast with a series of psychological data concerning our emotions. We will thus oppose Walton by considering a different approach to the paradox (cf. Szabó Gendler & Kovakovich 2005) that, by relying on this data, offers instead some good reasons to think that we cannot draw any justified distinction between genuine and pretend emotions.

2.4.1. *The paradox of fictional emotions*

The "paradox of fictional emotions" – as it has been labeled by Tamar Szabó Gendler and Karson Kovakovich (2005) – is typically described as a puzzle consisting of three claims, quite acceptable if considered one by one, but inconsistent if taken together. These claims can be expressed as follows (cf. Levinson 1990):

---

of "becoming a princess." From the cognitive point of view, however, this can only mean that, when I imagine "being a princess," I know that this content cannot be so easily realized as can be the content of "eating ice-cream." So, what seems to distinguish a genuine desire from a pretend desire is not their content, but at least some awareness about the probability that this content become reality.

(1) we all experience emotions towards fictional situations or characters;
(2) we all know that these situations or persons are fictional, meaning that they do not exist in the real world;
(3) but, for any rational agent, it seems true that her emotional response towards a given scenario can be genuine only provided that she believes the situation to be real.

All these statements clearly appeal to our common sense and seem undeniable, at least at first sight. We all experience some emotional reaction in reading a novel or watching a movie (this is, in fact, one of the main reasons why we create such things as novels and movies). At the same time, we ascribe the capacity to distinguish between what is fictional and what is real to every rational agent. Consequently, we end up with a problem: how can we have genuine emotions towards fiction if, at the same time, we are perfectly conscious that it is only fiction? And, if we do really have these genuine reactions, can we really call ourselves rational beings?

Traditional solutions to this paradox have tried to deny either the first claim, maintaining that our emotional responses towards fiction are not genuine ones (cf. Walton 1978, 1990, 1997), or the second claim, arguing that when we react emotionally to a fictional situation, it is because we momentarily suspend our belief in the fictionality of what we are paying attention to and believe, at least to a certain extent, that what is happening is real (this is the so-called "Illusion Theory," sustained by Anderson 1996 and Tan 1996). Only in recent years have some philosophers (cf. Szabó Gendler & Kovakovich 2005) argued that the puzzle is created neither by the first claim nor by the second, but rather by a third one: that is by the logical – or at least psychological – constraint that is put on the relation between our beliefs in the reality of a certain scenario and the possibility of having a genuine and rational emotional response towards it. In other words, although our emotional reactions can be mitigated or even stopped by the awareness that their object is fictional, these authors have claimed that it neither impossible nor irrational to respond with a genuine emotion towards a fictional scenario. On the contrary, what some experimental data seems to suggest, they have argued, is that the capability to respond genuinely to a certain possible scenario is a key cognitive ability and it is fundamental in order to be able to evaluate a certain situation and make the most rational choice. Before illustrating this position, however, let us first consider the other two solutions, in particular the most debated one: the theory of quasi-emotions, famously advanced by Kendall Walton.

2.4.2. *Quasi-emotions*

The reason we will focus mainly on the former solution is that the "Illusion Theory," to which we have hinted above, has encountered very little consensus among those philosophers who have discussed the paradox. The idea that, when we attend to fiction, we can somehow suspend our beliefs in the fictionality of a certain scenario and come to believe – even if in a weak sense of the word 'believing' – that what is happening in the fictional work is real seems highly implausible. Both the notion of a "suspension of disbelief" (in the fictionality of what we are paying attention to) and the notion of a "weak" or "partial belief" are very problematic. As it has been pointed out by Walton himself (cf. 1978: 7), if I had even only a partial belief that what I am seeing in a movie is real, my behavior would necessarily be influenced by it. For example, if I really suspected that the ferocious monster I am seeing on the screen is really invading the Earth and destroying everything on its path, it would be certainly rational on my part to call the police. Since I do not even consider this possibility, Walton argues, this is proof that I am constantly aware that what I see is fictional and, thus, that the Illusion Theory is false.

The theory proposed by Kendall Walton, on the contrary, has been one of the most influential. As said, Walton opted for denying the first claim and argued in favor of the idea that our emotions towards fiction are not genuine but rather only pretend ones. More precisely, what Walton claimed is that, although on the phenomenological and physiological level our emotions towards fiction can be similar or even indistinguishable from the emotions we feel towards real persons and events (1990: 202), these physiological and phenomenological reactions alone – what Walton calls *quasi-emotions* – cannot be considered genuine emotions, for they lack at least two fundamental elements: (1) the epistemic-cognitive state that constitutes their causal antecedent, and (2) the appropriate behavior, which instead constitutes their direct consequence. Walton illustrated his position with a famous example:

> Charles is watching a horror movie about a terrible green slime. He cringes in his seat as the slime oozes slowly but relentlessly over the earth destroying everything in its path. Soon a greasy head emerges from the undulating mass, and two beady eyes roll around, finally fixing on the camera. The slime, picking up speed, oozes on a new course straight toward the viewers. Charles emits a shriek and clutches desperately at his chair. Afterwards, still shaken, Charles confesses that he was 'terrified' of the slime. *Was* he? (1978: 5, Walton 1990: 196)

As one could expect, Walton's answer is negative. Charles is not a naïve spectator, Walton says; he knows very well that what is watching is only fictional and that the slime cannot endanger him, so, even if he has a phenomenal experience of fear – he sweats, his muscles are tensed, his heart is jumping, etc. – still we cannot rightly say "he feels fear" because Charles lacks a fundamental belief (the belief of being in danger).[6] As a consequence, he does not try escape from the theater, nor does he try to call the police or warn his family. In other words, his *quasi-emotion* has no effect on his deliberate behavior (1978: 7; 1990: 198).

By Walton's account, when Charles watches a movie, he is indeed engaged in a *game of make-believe*, similar to that of a baby who plays monster with his father (1990: 242). When the father pretends to be a ferocious monster who wants to eat him, the baby screams and runs to the next room but, although his screaming is almost involuntary, "he has a delighted grin on his face," Walton says, and he comes back for more. This is because the child is perfectly aware that the whole thing is just a game, and so he is not really, but only fictionally afraid (1990: *ibidem*). The same can be said about Charles's situation: Charles knows that he is watching a horror movie and that, as a result, he must feel afraid. His *quasi-fear* can thus be considered, Walton says, as his "psychological participation" in the game (1990: 241 ff.):

> Charles is participating psychologically in his game of make-believe. It is not true but fictional that he fears the slime. So of course he speaks of himself as being afraid of it. His speaking thus may itself constitute participation – verbal participation – in his game. It is fictional that he is afraid, and it is fictional that he says he is. (1990: 242)

2.4.3. *Against quasi-emotions*

Although Walton has always refused to embrace any particular theory of emotions, his account seems to be necessarily committed to a cognitive theory of emotions, according to which emotions are basically considered judgments or evaluative beliefs about things and situations. In this theory,

---

6   Walton (1990: 197) recognizes that in some special cases we can also feel genuine emotions towards fiction, but these are just those cases in which some naïve moviegoer takes the movie to be real. This happened, some say, at one of the first showings of Lumière: people took the movie to be real and ran out of the projection room terrified. In this case, they were truly terrified, because they really believed themselves in danger.

in fact, the epistemic-cognitive element plays a fundamental individuating role: for example, a state of fear is identified not only by the appropriate phenomenological and physiological reactions but, most importantly, by the fact of having a certain belief, the belief of being in danger, as its causal antecedent. In other words, in order to individuate a state of fear, it is not sufficient to have a certain physiological reaction accompanied by a certain phenomenological experience, but it is necessary to possess the appropriate kind of belief. Moreover, the cognitive theory of emotions also claims – as Walton does – that every emotional state must necessarily possess a certain motivational structure. That is, it must give rise to an appropriate behavior (for example, in the case of the green slime, the appropriate behavior could consist of calling the police and warning one's family). The cognitive theory of emotions, however, has received many criticisms, especially in the domains of evolutionary and developmental psychology (for a brief but exhaustive review cf. Morreall 1993).

Evolutionary psychology, on its part, has stressed the fact that the conception of an emotion typical of the cognitive theory contrasts with the role that emotions have played in our evolutionary history. If we consider the case of fear for example, fear presumably plays the biological function of protecting us by provoking certain physiological reactions that make us ready to react to potentially dangerous stimuli. In many cases, however, this emotion arises way before we have not only evaluated, but even recognized the stimulus as dangerous. This is clearly exemplified by the fear we feel on hearing a loud noise or on losing our balance: we react rapidly to the stimulus before having understood whether the stimulus is really dangerous or not. And this, far from being irrational, is perfectly understandable: to react readily to potentially dangerous stimuli is essential in order to survive, and discrimination, requiring time, can be an obstacle to a quick response. Or, to consider another fundamental emotion, we can think about our disgust if, while eating an apple, we bite into a bitter-tasting worm: we spit it out immediately and feel terribly disgusted without having any mental representation of what it could be (cf. Morreall 1993: 362). Again, this seems perfectly reasonable, since this slimy, bitter-tasting object could have actually been something dangerous.

What evolutionary psychology shows, then, is that our emotions – or at least the most fundamental ones, like fear, fright, disgust, anger, etc. – often occur without an epistemic-cognitive state as their causal antecedent. What is required in order to have some emotional reaction of this kind is not a conceptual content, but simply some perceptual information that has an immediate influence on our behavior.

Developmental psychology, in turn, has stressed the fact that, if we adopted the definition of an emotion given by the cognitive theory, we should conclude that infants and most animals do not have emotions, for they lack the correspondent epistemic-cognitive states. Infants and animals, in fact, do seem to fear without having a clear belief to be in danger, and this is also true in some cases for human adults. Typical examples are those in which we feel vicariously (that is, we fear not because we are endangered but because somebody else is, or we are happy not because something good has happened to us but rather to a friend of ours), or those in which we feel fear in spite of knowing well that we have nothing to be afraid of (think of the famous example proposed by Patricia Greenspan, according to which Frances, in consequence of being attacked by a rabid dog, fears all dogs, including old, toothless Fido, even though it is not possible to ascribe the belief that Fido is really dangerous to her, cf. Greenspan 1988: 17-20).

Important criticisms, however, can also be aimed at the second identifying condition for an emotion that the cognitive theory postulates: the manifest behavior that only genuine emotions are supposed to elicit. As seen, in Walton's view, the clearest proof that, in the case of fiction, our emotions are only pretend ones is that they do not give rise to the typical behavior that we would have in analogous real contexts. Walton compares Charles's fear with that of a person who is afraid to fly (1990: 198). In the latter case, although this person is aware that airplanes are the safest means of transport, she cannot help being afraid to fly and thus she avoids taking airplanes whenever she can. On the contrary, Walton says, Charles has voluntarily chosen to see a horror movie and remains seated in his chair until the end: his behavior is not coherent with his emotions, so we cannot say that Charles is really afraid but that it is only fictional that he is afraid.

To this kind of argument, however, one could reply that our real-life emotions also do not always bring us to an immediate deliberation and an overt behavior. If on one hand it is true that our emotional reactions towards fictional scenarios do not have the same effects that real scenarios typically have on our behavior, on the other hand, the idea that we can attribute a certain emotion to an individual only when she acts in the appropriate way possesses a behaviorist flavor that should make us suspicious. In particular, in the case of our emotions towards fiction, our behavior could be simply inhibited by the awareness of the fact that the depicted scenario is not real, but this does not amount to claiming that the emotion it causes lacks any motivating power. At the same time, our emotions in real life also do not always give rise to a specific behavior, but they too can be inhibited for several reasons.

To sum up, the problem with Walton's theory is that if we assume the strict identifying conditions for an emotion given by him, we find ourselves with a wide range of mental states that we would be inclined to define as genuine emotions but that instead turn out to be only pretend ones. In other words, if one relies on the classical cognitive theory of emotions and puts such strong constraints on the definition of a genuine emotion, then the concept of emotion becomes a very thin one, since one is compelled to exclude a large number of states that we normally consider genuine emotional reactions from this class. Not only our reactions towards fiction, but also fright, an irrational fear of a toothless dog, and even the instinctive (but non-conceptualized) fear exhibited by an infant placed on a cliff should all be considered only as cases of pretend emotions.

2.4.4. *Genuine rational fictional emotions*

As anticipated, Szabó Gendler and Kovakovich (2005) offered a new solution to the paradox of fictional emotions, arguing that the problem is created neither by the first nor by the second claim but rather by the constraints that the third claim puts on the genuineness and rationality of our emotions. In other words, what they have attempted to show is that having some emotional reaction towards a fictional scenario does not allow us to necessarily confirm either the pretendedness of this emotion or the irrationality of the subject who feels it. Interestingly, in order to demonstrate their thesis, they appealed to the theory of somatic markers presented above (cf. § 2.2), arguing that this theory allows us to conclude both the rationality and genuineness of our emotions towards all kinds of non-actual scenarios.

First of all, Szabó Gendler and Kovakovich claim that what Damasio has demonstrated with his experiment is that the capacity to feel an emotion towards a *possible, only-imagined* situation (as we have seen in Damasio's experiment, the imagined situation is the possible action to perform) is fundamental to take a rational decision and choose the most advantageous action in that situation. The people who are not able to have an emotional reaction towards an envisaged scenario typically act in a counterproductive way. In this sense, then, far from being an obstacle, our emotions towards imagined scenarios would be, instead, a fundamental ingredient of our practical rationality.

Second, they remark, nobody questions that the emotions that mark certain possible scenarios are genuine. But, if we admit this, then "fictional emotions" (the emotions we feel towards fictional scenarios) must also be so, for they share at least two crucial aspects with the former:

(1) their objects are non-actual;
(2) they are not directly tied to action.

In other words, Szabó Gendler and Kovakovich say, if we are disposed to consider our emotional reactions towards future or hypothetical situations as rational and genuine ones, why shouldn't we do the same with our responses towards fiction, given that fictional scenarios are also nothing but possible, non-actual situations?

Of course, one could decide to use the expression "fictional emotions" only for those emotions that are caused by a fictional scenario (by a story told in a book or by a movie) and to consider as "simulated emotions" the emotions we feel towards all other kinds of non-actual scenario, but in this case, Szabó Gendler and Kovakovich rightly observe, the debate would be reduced to a mere terminological dispute. On the contrary, once we recognize that the "simulated emotions" involved in our decision-making process and the emotions caused by fictional scenarios are both emotions felt towards *non-actual* scenarios, then, if we consider the former as genuine and rational, we will necessarily conclude that the latter are also nothing but *"genuine rational fictional* emotions."

2.5. *The impossibility of distinguishing genuine from pretend desires*

After having considered the arguments that have been given against the idea that we can speak of "pretend emotions" (or quasi-emotions, to use Walton's terminology), we can now come back to the question we started with: are pretend desires really *possible*? As we have seen, Carruthers explains our behavior in pretense by appealing to *genuine* – rather than pretend – desires, but what we want to stress is that he could not have done otherwise, since his notion of desire does not allow him to distinguish genuine from pretend desires. In fact, not only can pretend desires not be distinguished from genuine desires in their representational content (cf. *supra* § 2.4), but neither, it seems now, can they be distinguished from genuine desires in their emotional component.

More precisely, as we have seen, in the case of desires the emotional component is represented by a specific feeling – a feeling of pleasure – that can be well compared to other basic emotional reactions such as disgust or fear. The pleasure we feel in envisaging a certain possible scenario, in fact, arises far before we understand what could be pleasant in that scenario, and moreover, it typically arises in a completely unconscious way. Similarly to disgust or fear, then, this kind of pleasure also seems like a gut feeling, produced in an immediate and automatic way which does not require any specific cognitive or epistemic state as its causal antecedent and which does not necessarily lead to an overt behavior. Exactly like how, in normal cases, I am disgusted way before understanding what disgusts me, or like how I feel fear before understanding what endangers me, in much the same way I can feel pleasure when confronted with a certain (imaginary) scene before realizing what pleases me about that scene. The fact that it is a future or a mere fictional scenario that causes me pleasure is completely irrelevant with respect to the identifying conditions of the feeling itself.

Tracing a distinction between genuine and pretend desires by relying on an alleged distinction between a genuine and a pretend pleasure thus seems to be very hard. In this sense, we can conclude that the notion of desire proposed by Carruthers excludes *a priori* the existence of pretend desires, since both the identifying conditions for a desire are satisfied also by the desires we feel in fictional contexts. Our claim, however, is not intended to be a general one: we are ready to admit that, if one adopted a different conception of desire, one could distinguish genuine from pretend desires. This is the challenge that the sustainers of pretend desires are called to accept. If they want to maintain a simulative conception of the imagination, according to which we would be able to recreate both belief-like states and desire-like states, then they first have to give a plausible notion of desire that clearly indicates in what, exactly, genuine desires would differ from only imagined ones and how a subject could discriminate between them.

Summary of the chapter

In this chapter we have focused on our motivations to pretend. In particular, we have again opposed the theory proposed by Nichols and Stich – according to whom our behavior in pretense would be motivated by a genuine desire to act in accordance to the imagined scenario – and the recreativist account endorsed by Currie and Ravenscroft (2002) and Goldman (2006a, b) – according to whom pretense instead requires not only belief-like imaginings but also desire-like imaginings, that is, imaginings that play the same functional role as desires. As we have seen, the debate between the two positions has mainly focused on the question: are pretend desires really *necessary*? That is, can we explain our motivation to pretend and our emotional engagement with fiction only by postulating the existence of desire-like imaginings, or can we do without them? With respect to this question, we stand with Nichols and Stich and believe that the recourse to pretend desires is not so compelling.

As we have tried to show in the second part of the chapter, however, there is another, more fundamental question concerning pretend desires that still waits to be answered: are pretend desires really *possible*? The answer to this question depends, of course, on the notion of desire that one endorses. By the account that we favor, the "hybrid account" proposed by Peter Carruthers, we have shown that the notion of a pretend desire is simply impossible. In this sense, we have thus concluded, before arguing in favor of the existence of desire-like imaginings, recreativists should first of all specify which notion of desire they endorse and how it is possible to distinguish, on the basis of this notion, genuine from pretend desires.

IV.
METAREPRESENTATIONAL ABILITIES

One of the most well-known theories of pretense, developed at the end of the '80s by Alan Leslie, assigns a central role to our capacity for metarepresenting. As we will see in detail in the present chapter, this depends on the peculiar relation that, according to Leslie, exists between pretense and another important capacity, that is, mindreading. More precisely, Leslie claims, pretense can be seen as an early manifestation of the capacity to represent mental states: by representing someone as entertaining the attitude of pretending towards a certain imagined state of affairs, we would begin to conceptualize her or his behavior in a mentalistic way, as something which is caused by some inner state of mind.

Leslie's theory of pretense has received several criticisms, both on theoretical and empirical grounds. Famously, Perner (1991) has objected that the 'strong' notion of metarepresentation – understood as "a representation of a representation" – endorsed by Leslie cannot be possessed and mastered by young children, even if they are able to pretend: so, an ability for metarepresenting cannot be the key to explain our capacity for pretending. This has led Leslie to revise his conception of metarepresentation, but other authors, such as Nichols and Stich (2000), have also criticized this weakened notion and denied that younger children (less than 4-years old) can understand, not only the concept of a mental representation, but also concepts for mental attitudes such as 'belief' and 'pretense'.

Be that as it may, Leslie's theory has put at the centre of the debate the question of whether or not pretense requires some metarepresentational abilities and, if so, how these abilities should be conceived. With respect to this question, we can thus classify the theories of pretense in two main groups: the Behavioral theories and the Metarepresentational theories of pretense. According to the former group, in order to engage in and understand pretense, all we need is to understand that someone is behaving in a way that would be appropriate if p – a non-actual scenario – were the case (cf. Nichols & Stich 2000: 139). According to the latter, on the contrary, this is not enough: if all we needed in order to understand pretense, were to recognize that a certain behavior is not appropriate to the actual scenario but to a counterfactual one, then also mistakes, failures and accidents should be interpreted as cases of pretense (cf. e.g. Friedman & Leslie 2007). In order to recognize a behavior as an instance of pretense, the Metarepresentationalists claim, we must make use of a mentalistic concept, thus attributing to the pretender a peculiar mental attitude.

The chapter will develop as follows. In section 1 we will start by sketching out the main elements of Leslie's theory of pretense. Then, in section 2, we will illustrate the debate existing between the Metarepresentationalist and the Behavioral accounts of pretense. We will first take into consideration the criticisms that have been moved against Leslie's theory (§ 2.1), in particular by Perner (1991) and Nichols and Stich (2000), and then discuss those that Friedman and Leslie (2007) have recently developed against the competing account (§ 2.2). In section 3 we will examine the most well-known Behaviorist account, namely the famous theory of Mental Models proposed by Perner (1991) and developed by some of his followers (Olson 1993; Suddendorf 1999; Suddendorf & Whiten 2001). Meini and Voltolini (2009) have developed a convincing criticism against this account and offered a solution that tries to mediate between a purely Behaviorist account and a Metarepresentational one, proposing an only 'minimally metarepresentational theory' (§ 4), that we favor and that we will employ in our own account of pretense (cf. ch. 6).

1. *Leslie's theory of pretense*

1.1. *The problem of representational abuse*

In a paper written in 1987, in which the theory of pretense is presented for the first time, Leslie opens with a remark about the apparent oddness of the capacitty for pretending: although possibly funny, Leslie says, pretend play seems to be at best useless and at worst damaging:

> From an evolutionary point of view there ought to be a high premium on the veridicality of cognitive processes. The perceiving, thinking organism ought, as far as possible, to get things right. Yet pretense flies in the face of this fundamental principle. In pretense we deliberately distort reality. (1987: 412)

In this view, what Leslie calls "the capacity *for primary representation*" – the capacity "to represent aspects of the world in an accurate, faithful, and literal way", that the child seems to possess from birth and enhances through development – would risk being compromised by pretense (1987: 414). As Leslie recognizes, however, this does not happen, so the question is: why and how?

Pretense, Leslie remarks, seems to be characterized by the fact that the subject is dealing, at the very same time, with two representations: one is of the actual world, the other of the pretense scenario. To take, once again, Leslie's most famous example, when a child pretends that a banana is a telephone, she is not only representing that a certain perceived object is a banana, but also that that object is a telephone. Pretense, however, implies something more than having two distinct representations at once; it also implies the capacity to coordinate these representations and to establish a certain link between them. As Leslie remarks:

> It is this banana that I pretend is a telephone; it is this doll's face that I pretend is dirty. This must mean that pretend representations relate in specific ways to primary representations. The problem for current theory is to say what exactly this relation is. (1987: *ibidem*)

The problem is that, if both representations at stake during an episode of pretense were primary representations – that is, 'transparent' representations, possessing a direct semantic relation to the world – pretense would lead to what Leslie calls a *representational abuse* (1987: 414-415). In other words, the same representation would have, at the same time, two different referents, a banana and a telephone. Or, to put it differently, during an episode of pretense, the word 'telephone' would acquire a new meaning, thus coming to denote not only telephones, but also bananas (and, analogously, the correspondent mental symbol for telephones would start to be employed also for bananas). But this, of course, would be misleading, especially for a child who is still learning how language and mental representations work.

The problem of representational abuse, Leslie also remarks, is not confined to single terms' reference, but involves every form of pretense. As seen (cf. § I.1.4), according to Leslie there are three basic kinds of semantic relations that can hold between a representation and the world, and pretense can be conceived as a systematic distortion of one of these relations. In other words, for every semantic relation (reference, truth, existence), we can identify one form of pretense (object substitution pretense, attribution of pretend properties, imaginary objects pretense) that is obtained precisely from the distortion of that relation and, together with this distortion, we get a different risk of representational abuse (cf. 1987: 415-416). If pretending that a banana is a telephone is an example of the first kind of pretense (object substitution, which involves the risk of a deviant reference), pretending that a cup is full – when, in fact, it is empty – is an example of attribution of pretend properties, which implies the distortion of truth, so that *"empty* would now include situations in which cups contain water as well as situations in which cups contain nothing. Perhaps even worse, one could no longer infer from *the cup is empty* to *the cup contains nothing"* (1987: 415).

Finally, pretending that there is a spoon – when, instead, there is nothing – is a case of imaginary object pretense, in which the semantic relation concerned by the distortion produced in pretense is the entailment of existence. In this latter case, the risk associated with altering the existence relation consists in the fact that there is nothing to which the representation can make reference – no 'anchor' for the imaginary state (1987: *ibidem*).

Even more interesting, according to Leslie, is the fact that these problems of representational abuse do not concern only pretense, but also affect, in exactly the same manner, language and, more precisely, opaque contexts. In Leslie's opinion there is a clear isomorphism between the three forms of pretense sketched above and the three different forms of *opacity* that concern sentences embedded in attitude reports (that is, sentences introduced by *mental states terms* such as believe(s), desire(s), want(s), expect(s), and pretend(s)). When a sentence is embedded in an attitude report of the kind "x believes that...", Leslie remarks that in fact the normal semantic relations holding between this sentence and the world are not granted. For example, if we take the sentence "the Prime Minister of Britain lives at No. 10 Downing Street" and embed it in the report "Sarah-Jane believes that the Prime Minister of Britain lives at No. 10 Downing Street", we are no more entitled to substitute the definite description "the Prime Minister of Britain" with a co-referential expression like "David Cameron". As it is known, in fact, Sarah-Jane could ignore who is currently the Prime Minister of Britain or wrongly believe that it is, for example, Tony Blair. In this case, the attitude verb (believes) has an influence on language inasmuch as it suspends the normal reference relations and produces what Quine (1961) called "referential opacity". Something analogous also happens with a proposition such as "John believes that the cat is white", which, Leslie remarks, says nothing on whether or not the cat is really white: in this case what is suspended is the truth relation of the embedded proposition. Finally, a sentence like "the king of France is bald", when embedded in a report, no more implies the existence of the king of France, so the semantic relation concerned in this case is the entailment of existence (1987: 416).

According to Leslie, the isomorphism we have just illustrated is not at all accidental. On the contrary, this isomorphism is the clearest proof that the mechanism shared by these two different cognitive capacities – pretense and mindreading – is one and the same. More precisely, this isomorphism relies on the employment – both in pretense and mindreading – of a special kind of mental representation, that Leslie calls "M-representation".

1.2. *Decoupling and metarepresenting*

In order to avoid the risk of representational abuse, Leslie argues (1987: 417ff.; 1994: 217), we must suppose the existence of two further kinds of mental representations in addition to primary (i.e. transparent) representations, namely:
(1) *decoupled* representations;
(2) and *metarepresentations*.

Decoupled representations, Leslie says, are simply the opaque versions of primary representations: that is, they are first-order representations which have been *detached* from their normal input-output relations and *marked* in a special way, so that they can be distinguished and kept separate (*quarantined*) from representations of actual states of affairs. For example, as we have seen, in pretense the representation "that is a telephone" is detached from its normal input (the perception of a telephone) and is used to demonstratively refer to bananas (so it also has a different output). This means, according to Leslie, that this representation is marked in a special way, allowing the pretender to keep it distinct from her genuine perceptions.

In order to pretend, however, decoupled representations alone are not enough. In pretense, Leslie says, we not only need to decouple certain representations from their standard input and output relations, but we also need to embed them into a more complicated representational structure, which is precisely what Leslie calls a "metarepresentation" or – to distinguish it from Perner (1991)'s use of the term – an "M-representation". M-representations combine four kinds of information, respectively concerning (1994: 217):
(1) an agent;
(2) an informational relation (i.e. a mental attitude);
(3) an anchor (i.e. an aspect of the real situation);
(4) a description (i.e. an imaginary situation).
More precisely, an agent, who bears a real-world relation to some object or situation (the anchor), is represented, by means of an M-representation, as entertaining a mental attitude (the informational relation) towards the truth of a certain description (the imaginary situation). For example, when

a child observes her mother pretending that a banana is a telephone, what the child constructs, according to Leslie, is a representation of the form: "Mother PRETENDS (of) the banana (that) 'it is telephone'", i.e. she constructs a metarepresentation which depicts her mother as entertaining the attitude of pretending towards a certain content (the fact that the object in her hands is a telephone) (1994: 216).

Now, M-representations are precisely those representations that are produced, according to Leslie, by a specific module that subserves our capacity for mindreading. More precisely, as seen (cf. § I.3.1), on Leslie's account, the capacity for mindreading is subserved by a group of modules that he calls ToMM (the *Theory of Mind Mechanism*, cf. Baron-Cohen 1994). ToMM is a representational system which is part of our mental endowment and emerges at a certain stage in our development. The modules that constitute ToMM are devoted to the computation of different social stimuli and to the production of representations of different degrees of complexity. For example, the first module, called EDD (*Eye Direction Detector*), detects the presence of eye-like stimuli and from these inputs produces representations of dyadic relations of the kind <agent, SEE, me> or <agent, SEE, object>. EDD is present in a large number of species and emerges in humans around the age of 6 months. A slightly more complicated module, ID (*Intentionality Detector*), emerging after EDD, at around 9 months, is a perceptual device that computes visual, auditory and tactile stimuli concerning others' behavior, allowing the subject to attribute basic volitional states (goals). For example, from observing her father going towards a cake, an infant would be able to understand the father's behavior as an action directed towards a goal, and thus would be able to construct a representation of the kind <dad, WANT, cake>.

If EDD and ID produce dyadic representations (representations of a binary relation between an agent and an object, or an agent and the self), the module emerging between 9 and 14 months, called SAM (*Shared Attention Mechanism*), can build triadic representations of the kind "Mom *sees that I see* the cup". SAM, in other words, takes as input dyadic representations from ID and EDD, and embeds them into one another: for example, a dyadic representation as "I see a cup" is embedded within another dyadic representation, "Mom sees me", to produce the triadic representation "Mom sees that I see the cup". SAM thus allows us to understand what we call "joint attention behaviours", such as protodeclarative pointing and gaze monitoring.

Whereas this module is probably possessed also by some primates, the last module, which produces the most sophisticated representations, is probably present only in humans and develops between 2 and 4 years of age. This last module is precisely ToMM, the *Theory of Mind Mechanism*, which allows a subject to make sense of an agent's current behavior by producing not only triadic mental representations – representations of an agent as entertaining a certain mental attitude towards a certain content, as <agent, BELIEVES, p> or <agent, KNOWS, p> – but also what Leslie calls M-representations (Leslie 1994: 217ff.), that is, four-place representations which depict an agent as related not only to an aspect of the actual world, but also to the truth of a certain description (<agent, MENTAL ATTITUDE, real-world object, p>).

Now, this account of our capacity for mindreading explains why, according to Leslie (1987: 416), pretense must be considered an early manifestation of our capacity for mindreading: according to Leslie, pretend play would constitute one of the first steps in the development of a theory of mind precisely because in pretend play children are required for the first time to employ the most complicated kind of representations, that is, M-representations. Without M-representations, not only would the child not be able to engage in pretense, but she could also not understand pretense behaviors in others – an understanding which is, of course, a first step towards a full understanding of other minds. Against this claim, however, a long list of criticisms has been raised, as we will see in a moment.

2. *Metarepresentational* vs. *Behavioral theories of pretense*

2.1. *Problems for the Metarepresentational account*

As we have seen, the notion of 'metarepresentation' proposed by Leslie has been subject to several misunderstandings, which have originated, in particular, from Joseph Perner's (1991) interpretation of Leslie's claims.

Famously, Perner interpreted the notion of metarepresentation proposed by Leslie in the 'strong' sense used by Pylyshyn – to whom Leslie himself had made reference in his earlier papers – to mean a "representation of a representational relation" (cf. Leslie 1994: 216). Perner thus objected to Leslie's claim that, if children possessed a metarepresentational capacity in this strong sense, then they should be able to represent representations *qua* representations, and thus we should ascribe to them the mastering of the *concept* of representation. But, Perner claimed, children do not acquire this concept before the age of 4, as demonstrated by the results obtained with the false-belief task[1], whereas they

---

1   The false-belief task, originally ideated by Wimmer and Perner (1983), is considered a decisive proof in order to establish whether or not a child has acquired

start to engage in and understand pretense way before that age. So, if a full-blown metarepresentational ability were really required in order to pretend, children should not be able to pretend until the age of 4.

In his following works, Leslie thus adopted a weaker notion of metarepresentation, under which a metarepresentation would simply represent an agent as entertaining a certain *mental attitude* (what Leslie calls an "informational relation") towards the truth of a certain description. For example, as seen above (cf. § 1.2), by means of a metarepresentation the child would represent her mother as entertaining the attitude of *pretending* towards the possible state-of-affairs "this is a telephone". But, according to Leslie, attributing a mental attitude like pretending does not imply understanding a mental attitude as a mental representation:

> This is not the same as saying that a metarepresentation represents a mental state as *being a mental state* (or as *being a representation* or *as being a mental representation*). If a metarepresentation did any of these, then the earlier examples would look something like, I PRETEND THE BANANA "IT IS A TELEPHONE" AND PRETENDING IS A MENTAL STATE / MENTAL REPRESENTATION. Instead, a metarepresentation simply represents pretending as *pretending*. There has been some confusion about this following Perner's (1991) arguments that the term metarepresentation *must* be used to mean: a representation of a mental state as being a mental representation. We see no reason to accept this stricture. (Friedman & Leslie 2007: 109)

As one can see from this quotation, according to Leslie, attributing a state of pretense would simply amount to attributing a certain property – that of holding an informational relation to a certain content – to an agent, but this attribution would not require the subject to conceptualize this property (the attitude) as a mental state, i.e. as a mental representation of some kind.

Important criticisms, however, have also been raised against this weakened notion of pretense. In particular, Nichols and Stich (2000) have claimed that, even if Leslie's theory does not compel us to attribute to the pretending child the mastering of the concept of representation, still it compels us to grant that she masters at least some mentalistic concepts, such as those of 'belief' and 'pretense'. But, the authors have claimed, this knowledge is also too much for a young child.

---

the capacity for mindreading. This task requires that the child understands that a representation of the world can differ from how the world really is.

More precisely, Nichols and Stich have conceptualized the distance existing between their own theory and Leslie's in the following terms. Leslie's theory of pretense, they say, can be split into two distinct claims:
(1) the proposal that the representations that subserve pretense must be 'marked' in a specific way, in order to avoid that they be confused with primary representations;
(2) the idea that these representations – that Leslie calls "decoupled representations" – must be embedded in a higher-order structure, the metarepresentation or M-representation, which depicts the informational relation existing between an agent and a certain decoupled representation.

Now, the authors claim, whereas the first part of Leslie's theory is perfectly compatible with their own, the second is not and must be rejected. The first claim, in fact, aims to explain the cognitive quarantine of our pretend representations, for which, as seen below, Nichols and Stich have envisaged a special box, the Possible Worlds Box:

> to claim that a class of representations is specially marked and that the marking has important consequences for how the representations are treated is another way of saying that marked representations and unmarked representations are functionally different. Since the "box" metaphor is just a notational device for distinguishing representations that have systematically different functional or computational properties, Leslie's hypothesis that representational abuse is avoided because the representations subserving pretense are "quarantined" or "marked off" (Leslie, 1987, p. 415) is equivalent to claiming, as we do in our theory, that pretense-subserving representations are in a box of their own. (Nichols & Stich 2000: 136)

Saying that decoupled representations are marked in a special way would thus amount to saying, according to Nichols and Stich's interpretation, that these representations have a different functional role within the mind. As seen, however, according to Leslie, decoupled representations are not enough in order to explain our engagement with pretense. What we employ during an episode of pretense – both when we are involved in the game or when we interpret it – is a more complicated metarepresentational structure of the form "X *pretend(s)* that *p*", in which the decoupled representation with content *p* is embedded. For example, when the child plays the tea-party scenario with the experimenter, she forms a representation with content "we *pretend* that that cup is full of tea" – which contains the decoupled representation "that cup is full of tea" – and it is this metarepresentation – and not merely the decoupled representation embedded in it – that guides her behavior. In other words, according to Leslie's view, those representations that subserve pretense are not simply decoupled representations, but rather, metarepresentations. This explains why Leslie does not accept the 'boxology' introduced by Nichols and Stich or, more precisely, the existence of a Possible Worlds Box:

> According to Leslie, in terms of boxology, there is no such thing as the 'pretend box', and thus no such thing as simply 'having a pretend'. Instead, pretending is a special case of placing a representation in the 'belief box', where the representation says in effect, 'someone is pretending such and such.' (Nichols *et al.* 1996: 56)

To put it differently, understanding and engaging in pretense means, for Leslie, to possess certain special beliefs in one's own Belief Box, some beliefs with form "Y *pretend(s)* that *p*" (for example, "I *pretend* that *p*", or "x is *pretending* that *q*"). On the contrary, Nichols and Stich distinguish the representations that guide our behavior in pretense from those by means of which we represent ourselves, or someone else, as pretending. When I pretend – e.g. when I pretend that this cup contains tea – Nichols and Stich say, I simply have a representation in the PWB whose content is roughly the fact that "this cup contains tea". This pretend representation, together with some genuine desire of mine (e.g. the desire to drink some tea) is what motivates my behavior (thus inducing me to take the cup and pretend to drink). So, Nichols and Stich claim (2000: 137), my pretense could proceed, at least in principle, even if I had no beliefs about my pretense, that is, no beliefs of the form "I *am pretending* that such and such", and this grants that also people (or animals) who do not possess the concept of pretense can pretend. Of course, adults and older children can monitor their own pretense and form beliefs about what they are pretending. So, if one reflects about what she is doing or another person is doing, a representation with content "I *am pretending* that such and such" or "he *is pretending* that such and such" will come up in one's Belief Box. This, however, is not necessary in order to be able to pretend; it is necessary only in order to understand pretense, that is, in order to conceptualize one's own or another's behavior as a certain kind of behavior, guided by a certain mental attitude.

Nichols and Stich have also considered the argumentations that Leslie has offered in support of his theory and criticized three main claims that Leslie has made in favor of his Metarepresentational account. The first – and perhaps most well-known – reason provided by Leslie is that only the Metarepresentational account can explain the phenomenon that he calls "yoking" (cf. §I.1.3), namely, the fact that the ability to engage in solitary pretense emerges exactly at the same time as the capacities to engage in pretense with other people and to understand pretense in others. According to Leslie, this empirical fact shows that one and the same structure – a metarepresentation – subserves both our capacity to engage in pretense and to understand pretense in others (cf. 1987: 415-416; 1994: 216). If this were not the case, Leslie argues, we would expect that children first learn to pretend alone – an activity which seems to be less demanding – and only later come to understand pretense in others and to engage in collective games of make-believe.

As observed by Nichols and Stich, by Leslie's account a child who understands that someone is pretending not only understands that the person in question *is behaving in a way that would be appropriate if* p *were the case* (this is the Behavioral definition of pretense), but she understands that this person "is behaving in a way that would be appropriate if p were the case *because she is in a particular mental state, viz. pretending that p*" (2000: 139). However, this mentalistic account of pretense, Nichols and Stich remark, has been put into question by several empirical tests.

One of the most famous among these studies was conduced by Angeline Lillard (1993). In this experiment, children were presented with a troll doll, named Moe, who happened to be hopping like a kangaroo. Children, however, were told that Moe knew nothing about kangaroos and then asked whether or not Moe was pretending to be a kangaroo. The majority of children under 6 years of age answered affirmatively, claiming that Moe was indeed pretending to be a kangaroo, even if he had no knowledge about this animal.[2] From this and subsequent experiments[3] Lillard thus concluded that children under the age of 6 seldom understand pretense in mentalistic

---

2   More precisely, Lillard says (2001: 500), over many such experiments conducted in several laboratories, 4-year-olds' performance averaged 26% correct (over 23 experiments) and 5-year-olds' 46% (over 11 experiments). Moreover, the percentage of children who pass the task increases by about 15% per year, between the age of 4 and 8.

3   The results obtained by Lillard 1993 were later criticized, in particular because the mental state attributed to the pretending subject (i.e. Moe's knowledge) was at odds with his behavior. In other words, the troll acted like a kangaroo but did not know what a kangaroo is: an idea that could be quite puzzling for a child. Other tests have thus aimed to verify whether the experimental settings in which the action performed is consistent with the agent's mental state can help the child to understand pretense in mentalistic terms. What these tests have shown is that 3 year-olds understand pretense at least as something which is not real, but they are not able to distinguish cases of pretense from other kinds of behavior, such as acting in error, failures, etc. (cf. Lillard 2001: 499-508).

terms and rather tend to think of pretending as *behaving-as-if* (cf. Lillard 1993b, 1994, 2001).

Subsequent experiments have shown that children under the age of 4 are inclined to interpret all actions that do not correspond to the way the world actually is as pretense. This has emerged very clearly in an experiment conduced by Perner and colleagues (1994). In this test, children were shown a doll who put a carrot into an empty cage (the doll could not see the content of the cage). In one condition, however, the doll had previously seen that there was a rabbit inside (so, she believed that there was a rabbit inside); in the other, she knew that there was no rabbit in the cage. Children were then asked whether the character really thought that there was a rabbit or was just pretending. Whereas 3-year-olds claimed that the doll was just pretending, in both cases, 4-year-olds were able to discriminate between cases of true pretense and cases of false belief. This, again, contrasts with the idea, sustained by Leslie, that children from the age of 2 would be able to master the mentalistic concept of pretense and to distinguish episodes of pretense from other kinds of behaviors.

The second reason to sustain a Metarepresentational account is tied, instead, to the close parallel that, according to Leslie, exists between the semantic properties of mental states expressions – such as 'believe(s)', 'desire(s)', etc. – and the three basic forms of pretense (cf. § 1.1). As we have seen, according to his view, this parallel is not at all accidental, but depends on the fact that in all these cases – both when we attribute an epistemic state and when we attribute a state of pretense to a subject – we are employing a certain metarepresentational structure – an M-representation – which is responsible for the referential opacity of the embedded representation.

However, Nichols and Stich observe (2000: 141) that positing this parallel between pretending and other mental states, has an unwelcome consequence, for:

> if it is plausible to suppose that the mental representation subserving the pretense that a certain cup contains tea has the form I PRETEND "this empty cup contains tea", then, given the parallels we have noted, the mental representation subserving the belief that this cup contains tea should be I BELIEVE this cup contains tea, and the mental representation subserving the desire that it rain tomorrow should be I DESIRE that it rain tomorrow. And if this were the case, then it would be impossible to believe anything without having the concept of belief, and impossible to desire anything without having the concept of desire. So any organism that had any beliefs and desires at all would have to have these concepts and thus at least the beginnings of a theory of mind.

Also, this argument turns out to be highly implausible, since the fact of entertaining a certain mental state would necessarily imply the fact of being aware of that state, that is, of being aware of the kind of state we are entertaining at a given moment.

Finally, the third argument makes appeal to an important discovery made by Baron-Cohen, Leslie and Frith (1985), which concerns children affected by autism. Autistic children typically show a pair of significant (and plausibly correlated) deficits: on one hand, they rarely engage in pretend play; on the other hand, they also show an impairment in understanding false-belief tasks and other tasks which are employed in order to establish one's ability at reading minds. This evidence has been interpreted by Leslie (cf. 1987: 423-424) as a further confirmation of the relation existing between pretense and mindreading. More precisely, what Leslie supposes is that both deficits would be due to an impairment of the decoupling mechanism, i.e. of the mechanism by means of which our representations of non-actual scenarios are decoupled from their standard input and output relations and marked in a special way, in order to avoid confusing them with primary representations.

Although Nichols and Stich agree with Leslie's hypothesis (about the possible impairment of the decoupling mechanism), they nevertheless observe that this kind of argument is completely useless for demonstrating the need for a metarepresentational structure. As the authors say (2000: 141-142):

> If the decoupler (or the system that puts representations into the PWB) is impaired then we would expect to find deficits in the ability to pretend, no matter what account one favors about the exact form of the representations that subserve pretense.

So, the authors conclude, if the first two arguments in favor of the Metarepresentational account can be contrasted both on theoretical and empirical grounds, the third is simply of no help. Let us consider, then, the replies that Leslie has formulated against the competing, Behavioral account.

2.2. *Problems for the Behavioral account*

In a recent paper, Friedman and Leslie (2007) have replied to the criticisms moved against the Metarepresentational account by developing an equally detailed criticism of the Behavioral theories of pretense.

According to the authors, the general problem with the Behavioral accounts is that they consider the capacities for engaging in and understanding pretense as two quite distinct abilities, which rely on different mental states and mechanisms. For example, according to Nichols and Stich's view, whereas the capacity to engage in pretense would depend on the capacity to entertain suppositions – i.e. to entertain representations of non-actual states of affairs and keep them quarantined from those of actual states of the world – the capacity to understand pretense in others would rely, rather, on an ability to recognize that someone *is behaving in a way that would be appropriate if* p *(a certain state of affairs) were true*. But, Friedman and Leslie claim, if this Behavioral account is able to satisfactorily explain the former capacity – that is, how the child can engage in pretense – it equally fails to satisfactorily explain the latter, that is, how the child can understand pretense in others. The critical points concluded by the authors are basically three:

(1) if one adopts a Behavioral theory of pretense, then there is plenty of behaviors that should be recognized by children as pretense, although they are not;

(2) the Behavioral account cannot grant that the child who observes a pretense behavior will not get confused, in particular about the function of the objects used in pretense;

(3) finally, the Behavioral theory cannot explain certain cases of object substitution pretense.

Let us start with the first.

According to Friedman and Leslie, the major problem with the Behavioral account is that its description of a pretense behavior – as "behaving in a way that would be appropriate if *p* were the case" – is too broad and can be applied to a huge number of behaviors that are not true cases of pretense (2007: 210-211). In other words, if children understood all behaviors which are inappropriate to the actual state of affairs as cases of pretense, then also mistakes, failures and accidents would be classified as pretense behaviors. For example, Friedman and Leslie say, if Sally's mother mistook an apple-shaped candle for a real apple and behaved accordingly, e.g. trying to bite into the apple-shaped candle, we should expect Sally to understand her mother's behavior as pretense (2007: 211).

To be sure, the authors recognize, this prediction has been experimentally tested by some psychologists, who have found that young children actually take some cases of mistaken behavior for pretense (cf. the experiment by Perner *et al.* 1994, cited above, but also Lillard 2001: 504-505). But, Friedman and Leslie reply, even if in some cases mistaken behaviors are interpreted as instances of pretense, Behavioralists underestimate the pervasiveness of this phenomenon. Nearly every kind of action, in fact, could be interpreted as an instance of pretense to the extent to which the child recognizes a similarity between the action performed and some other behavior:

> All that is required is that the child should be able to identify a similarity between one thing and another. Now, for any arbitrary x and y, x is similar to y on some dimension. Similarity and similarity detection is so ubiquitous that Behavioral theory predicts that children should mistake virtually all behaviors for pretense. However, we know of no evidence to suggest that children do vastly over-interpret other people's behavior as pretense. So something is missing from Behavioral theory. (2007: 111)

The example suggested by Friedman and Leslie is the following. Suppose that Sally's mother, having at her disposal a piece of charcoal, decides to draw something on a piece of paper. In this case, Sally might remark the similarity between the charcoal and a crayon and conceptualize her mother's behavior as "mom is behaving in a way that would be appropriate if the charcoal were a crayon", and so she would probably judge this behavior as an instance of pretense – when, instead, it is not (it is, rather, a case of functional play, cf. § I.1.1).

This example, however, is not as problematic as Friedman and Leslie seem to think. In particular, it is doubtful, in my view, that Sally should really conceptualize her mother's behavior in the way illustrated above. More precisely, I do not see why the child should judge that behavior as inappropriate to the actual scenario: if her mother's goal is to make a drawing, then, using a charcoal is a perfectly appropriate behavior – or, at least, it is a non-conventional but still appropriate behavior. As a consequence, Sally should not judge the action as appropriate to a counterfactual scenario (one in which the charcoal is a crayon) but rather, she should judge it as appropriate to the actual scenario because, as said, the charcoal *is really* a kind of crayon (it can really serve a crayon's function).

Friedman and Leslie also rule out the possibility, for the Behavioral account, to appeal to 'manner cues', i.e. to all those behaviors – such as intonation, exaggerated motions, 'knowing looks' and smiles, etc. – that can help the child to understand that certain behaviors are pretend ones. In other words, a Behaviorist could argue that the reason why only some behaviors (among all those behaviors which are not appropriate to the actual scenario) are considered cases of pretense is that in these cases the child recognizes some cues from which she can infer that she is faced with an episode of pretense. Friedman and Leslie, however, argue that the 'manner cues' solution turns out to be in contradiction with the Behavioral description.

Take again the case of Sally's mother, and imagine that she uses, this time, a stone as a crayon, and suppose that, while pretending to draw, the mother is making some exaggerated drawing motions, that she smiles, etc.:

> all these exaggerations, mannerisms, and the lack of any real drawing actually decrease the extent to which *she behaves in a way appropriate to if the stone were a crayon*. Attending to manner cues will not therefore save the Behavioral theory; instead manner cues add to its difficulties. (2007: 112)

According to the authors, then, the problem is that these kinds of cues, added to a pretending behavior, would make the behavior less appropriate, so that, the more manner cues are added, the less the child should be able to understand that behavior as appropriate to a certain imagined situation, and thus to recognize it as an instance of pretense. This problem, Friedman and Leslie remark, does not arise in their theory, since in this case the child does not have to judge the appropriateness of someone's behavior. Manner cues by this account are simply cues that, when detected, induce the child to apply the mentalistic concept of pretense to the action concerned.

This objection, however, does not seem to be charitable enough. If it is true that sometimes pretense behaviors can be strange and do not perfectly mirror their genuine counterparts, the notion of 'appropriateness' must necessarily be an elastic one. For every scenario, in fact, we can certainly envisage a long series of behaviors which are all – more or less – appropriate to the situation. Moreover, all the cues that characterize a pretense episode could be interpreted in the perspective of relevance theory: in other words, by means of a different intonation, or exaggerated movements, the child would be induced to understand that the pretender is doing something interesting, e.g. that she is not merely moving a stone over the paper, but that her behavior requires a more sophisticated understanding from the child.

Even less convincing, in my view, is the second criticism advanced against the Behavioral account. According to Friedman and Leslie (2007: 214), when a child observes an episode of pretense, there are two possible sources of confusion. The first derives from the fact that the child must have some representations of a non-actual scenario and keep them separate from his or her genuine representations. Behavioral theories, however, do not encounter problems explaining this fact, since they all envisage some form of decoupling, as, for example, the quarantine of pretend representations in the PWB (Nichols & Stich 2000).

Another source of confusion derives, instead, from the fact that, since in pretense a banana is used as a telephone, this could induce the child to generalize and think that all bananas – and not only that banana in particular

– *should* be treated as telephones. If, from observing an adult using a piece of charcoal as a crayon, the child comes to believe that pieces of charcoal can really be used as crayons, Friedman and Leslie argue, why shouldn't they come to believe that bananas can really be used as telephones? The Metarepresentational account, the authors claim, can easily explain this situation: since Sally represents her mother as *pretending*, then she does not believe that bananas can be used as telephones; in other words, the mastering of the concept of pretense allows her to rule out the possibility that her mother could be illustrating, by her behavior, a possible, alternative function of bananas (2007: *ibidem*).

In my view, however, this kind of objection is completely off target. First of all, Friedman and Leslie make an appeal to the wrong example, by comparing the case of a banana used as a telephone – which is a real case of pretense – with the case of a piece of charcoal used as a crayon – which, as recognized by the authors themselves (cf. 2007: 111), is not a genuine example of pretense, but rather a case of functional play. As I have already remarked, by using a piece of charcoal to draw, the mother is not pretending to draw: she is really drawing and, by doing so, she is showing her child a possible function of a piece of charcoal. But, if this is so, then we can easily predict that, on future occasions, the child will exploit this knowledge, and thus will use pieces of charcoal as crayons. The same, of course, cannot happen in the case of a banana used like a telephone. According to the Behavioral account, in fact, when we observe a genuine episode of pretense, what we detect is a behavior which is not appropriate to the actual situation but, rather, to a non-actual one. When the child observes mom using the banana as a telephone, she recognizes a behavior – making a telephone call – that is not appropriate towards bananas, but only towards telephones. Whereas a charcoal can well be considered as a (special kind of) crayon, a banana will never serve the purpose of a telephone. So, how can a child be induced, from pretense, to think that bananas should be treated as telephones?

Thirdly, according to Friedman and Leslie, the Behavioral account seems to face some significant difficulties explaining certain cases of object substitution pretense. The example proposed by Friedman and Leslie is the following:

> Suppose Sally engages in object substitution pretense by pretending that a pencil is a car: she may push the pencil along a table top to pretend that the pencil/car is driving along. She may also make engine noises, such as "vroom, vroom", to pretend that the pencil as car is making these noises. According to the Behavioral theory, Sally is behaving in a way that would be appropriate if

the pencil really were a car. But is she? No. If the pencil *were* a car then Sally would hardly push it across a table or make engine noises! Handling, pushing, and making "vroom" noises are not appropriate behaviors when dealing with a *real* car. Instead, appropriate behaviors for dealing with a real car include opening its doors, getting inside or, if one is very young, being placed inside, sitting still, and looking out the window. (2007: 115)

In order to get around this problem, Friedman and Leslie claim, the Behavioral account needs to be extended. Behavioralists could thus postulate that, according to their theory, someone is pretending *either* when she acts in a way that would be appropriate if *x* were a *y*, *or* when she makes *x* move in a way that would be appropriate if *x* were a *y* (2007: 116).

As the authors remark, this is the solution adopted e.g. by Lillard (1993a: 357), but it seems to be an *ad hoc* solution, something that has been added to the original theory just to solve the specific problems posed by these cases of pretense. Moreover, Friedman and Leslie observe, this kind of solution explains only one aspect of the above example – the fact that the child moves the object – but not, for instance, the sound effects that she produces. In order to also explain this aspect of pretense, other addenda would be required (for a discussion, cf. 2007: 116-117).

Contrary to Friedman and Leslie, however, I think that the right way to solve this problem is not that of modifying the Behavioral definition of pretense. Rather, I think that it is necessary to recognize, first of all, that all these kinds of examples rest on a mistake about what should be considered part of the context of pretense and what should not. In other words, the problem, in my view, consists in the fact that these behaviors – moving an object, emitting sounds – are usually considered pretense behaviors, that is, they are considered part of the context of pretense, when in fact they are not. On the contrary, I think that they should be considered instrumental behaviors, that is, behaviors which are out of the context of pretense but whose aim is to produce some facts, which themselves are part of the context of pretense.

For example, by moving the pencil, Sally is making the pencil move in a way that would be appropriate if the pencil were a car, and, much the same way, by making noises, Sally is producing sounds that would be appropriate to a moving car. The pencil's movement is certainly part of the pretense: it stands for the car's movement, and the same is true for the sounds, which stand for the sounds made by the car. But the movements made by Sally in order to produce the pencil's movement and the sounds, *her own* behaviors, are not part of the context of pretense. So, I want to claim, the right way to describe an example like the one above is to say that the pencil

– and not Sally herself – is behaving in a way that would be appropriate if the pencil were a car.

To sum up, from the review of the debate between Metarepresentationalists and Behavioralists, we can provisionally conclude that the arguments provided by the latter seem to be less problematic, and thus more convincing, than those provided by the former. A Metarepresentational account such as that proposed by Leslie, even in its weak version, seems to still be too demanding for young children. As we will see in detail in the next section (§ 3), however, a Behavioral account also has to face some problems when it comes to explaining how, exactly, our pretend representations can be quarantined from our genuine representations. In particular, we will take into consideration the Behavioral account of pretense famously proposed by Perner (1991) – the so-called "Theory of Mental Models" – and developed by some of his followers, which represents a radically anti-metarepresentationalist position. We will try to show the kind of problems it encounters, finally offering a possible solution, which consists of adopting a new and very 'thin' conception of what a metarepresentational ability is (§ 4).

3. *Perner and the Pernerians: the multiple models theory and the collating mind*

3.1. *The multiple models theory*

In order to understand Perner's proposal, it is useful to start with his notion of a *model*, that he introduces, as a kind of metaphor, to explain how mental representations work.

As an example of what a model is, Perner takes military sandboxes, which are employed in the army in order to represent the situation on the battlefield and plan new strategies (1991: 25). We can thus imagine one of these sandboxes, containing, besides the sand, some little sticks and other pieces of wood. The sand is shaped in the same way the battlefield is: little reliefs in the sand stand for the hills on the battlefield, whereas furrows stand for ditches; moreover, sticks stand for soldiers and blocks of wood for tanks, and also the spatial distances in the sandbox reflect those in the battlefield (1991: *ibidem*). So, if we suppose that the scouts have made no errors in construing the model (e.g. in estimating the distances between the tanks and the military target, or in counting the number of soldiers displaced on the field), we can conclude that the general who interprets the model will get a truthful picture of an actual state of affairs, that is the situation holding at the battlefield.

Now, the model constituted by the sandbox is, of course, a metaphor of what a mental representation is. A representation, according to Perner, is a *medium* (i.e. a kind of mental picture) which is related to a certain content (the depicted). "Representations", Perner says, "represent something *as being a certain way*" (1991: 15). In this sense, a sandbox can be seen as a tridimensional picture which is related to a certain content (the battlefield) and depicts it as being a certain way (e.g. with a certain number of soldiers and tanks, etc.).

Not all representations, however, have the same functional role. Some kinds of states, such as seeing, knowing, or believing, are *cognitive* or *epistemic* states, meant to reflect actual states of affairs – "how the world really is", Perner says – but other states represent, instead, possible or desirable scenarios. Within this group we can find both *conative* states, such as desires, hopes, or goals, and other *hypothetical* states, such as suppositions and pretenses.

Now, the problem is that in a large number of situations we entertain different kinds of representations at the same time. For example, we could want to compare our present situation with a past one; or, when we have to make a decision, we combine a belief of ours with a desire, thus representing not only an actual state of affairs, but also some possible, desirable situation; finally, as already seen, in pretense we must deal at the same time with a representation of reality and with one of an imaginary situation. Briefly, we can list several occasions in our lives which require that we deal with *multiple models* and the problem is always: how can we keep these representations distinct when they occur in our mind at the same time? Or, similarly, how can a general know whether the model he or she is considering is a model of the actual situation at the battlefield, rather than a model of a future scenario, that is, the representation of a possible strategy to implement? As Perner says (1991: 33),

> The model "s-in-d" specifies the situation as one where *the soldier is inside his ditch*, but it leaves open whether this *is* the situation out on the battlefield, whether it *was* the situation there, or whether it is purely hypothetical. In other words, the model's internal structure leaves open what the referent is. However, for correct use of the model this needs to be specified. How can this be done?

A plausible solution, Perner says (1991: 38), would seem to be appealing to our metarepresentational ability, thus claiming that, when we entertain multiple models, we are not only able to represent different situations at the same time, but we are also able to represent the relationship existing between every model and the content represented by the model itself. To put it differently, when dealing with different kinds of representations, we would be able not only to represent different contents, but also to represent our representations *qua* representations (1991: 35, 41). According to Perner, however, this solution has to be rejected since it leads to an infinite regress (1991: 38):

> To properly model that a model represents the real situation, one needs a model of the real situation, but for that model the same problem arises, namely, how to mark that it represents the real situation. To answer this question metarepresentationally by representing that this model represents the real situation raises the same question yet again, and so on ad infinitum.

In other words, if I represent a certain representation as the representation of an actual situation, then I will have to represent that situation as an actual one. That is, I will have to construct another model for that situation and to 'mark' that model as an actual one. But this will require, again, another model, and so on *ad infinitum*.

The only way to avoid this regress, Perner says, is to abandon the Metarepresentational account and to opt for another account, which simply makes appeal to the *internal function* of our representations. Exactly as a military apparatus relies on certain processes – e.g. the work done by its scouts – as reliable sources of intelligence, Perner says, biological organisms have evolved with perception as a reliable source of information:

> Introspectively, we know that what we see *is* real. We do not make that assumption because, having access to a theory of the process of perception, we have decided that this process is reliable and therefore good for composing models of reality. No, we just rely on perception. It imposes itself as reality. In other words, we do not *inspect* our perceptual data base to infer reality but use it – quite transparently – by letting ourselves be guided by it with respect to reality. (1991: *ibidem*)

What Perner seems to suggest here is simply the fact that we do not decide that certain representations are representations of actual situations, nor do we have to recognize them as such. They simply are representations of the actual situation because we treat them as such, "by letting ourselves be guided by them with respect to reality".

As I will try to show in detail in the next paragraphs, however, this solution is quite unsatisfying. More precisely, I agree with Meini and Voltolini (2010) that, if we adopt the mental models theory, we will not be able to discriminate between the cognitive situation of a pretender and similar cognitive situations, such as that of a dissociated subject. Before discussing this point, however, let us first consider the criticisms that Meini and Voltolini have moved against some Pernerian accounts, which have tried to solve this problem with Perner's original theory.

3.2. *The collating mind*

As stated by Meini and Voltolini (2010), followers of Perner (Olson 1993; Suddendorf 1999; Suddendorf & Whiten 2001) who have adopted his multiple models account, have also recognized the need for a collating mind, i.e. for a mind capable of comparing and assembling states belonging to different representational models. Still, these authors have kept faithful to Perner to the extent to which they have claimed that this collating mind needs not be metarepresentational.

Meini and Voltolini have challenged this view by sustaining the following three claims:

> a) the job performed by the collating mind, as described by its sustainers, is not enough in order for someone to pretend; b) even if, contrary to fact, it were enough, the collating mind would be metarepresentational in the same, minimal, sense in which, in our account, the pretending subject is [...]; c) the reason why the collating mind, or our pretending mind for that matters, is not understood by those authors to be metarepresentational is that they entertain a poorly articulated concept of metarepresentation. (2010: 44)

First of all, as claimed by Meini and Voltolini, it is not clear at all what kind of job the collating mind would do. More precisely, we can distinguish at least two different theories. According to the first, sustained by Whiten and Suddendorf (2001), the goal of the collating mind would be combining the two representations activated in the real and the imaginary model, respectively, into a third representation. For example, by combining the representation "this is a banana" with the representation "this is a telephone", the collating mind would produce a representation with content "this banana is a telephone". But, Meini and Voltolini (2010: *ibidem*) object, since the concept of banana is semantically inert within the representation "this banana is a telephone" – it has been decoupled from its standard inputs and outputs, to use Leslie's terminology –, then this representation is destined to collapse on the second ("this is a telephone").

According to another interpretation, given by Olson (1993), the collating representation would compare, instead, the real object represented in the reality model with that represented in the imaginary model. The collating representation would thus take the form: "the banana stands for the telephone". This interpretation, however, the authors remark, is very far from Perner, since, according to him, the notion of pretending is different and not reducible to that of a symbolic function ("something standing for something else", cf. Perner's objections to Piaget in Perner 1991: 56ff.). Moreover, as seen, some cases of pretense (e.g. pretending that there is a hat on Teddy's head, when, instead, there is nothing) are not describable as cases in which something stands for something else. So, it is difficult to see which kind of representation the collating mind could produce in these cases (2010: 45).

Finally, the authors say, at least Olson's interpretation of the collating mind is necessarily metarepresentational. In fact, if the collating representation represents something as *standing for* something else, then it represents the fact that something *represents* something else. Still, the authors claim, saying that the content of the representation produced by the collating mind is metarepresentational does not amount to saying that it is a metarepresentation in the strong sense meant by Perner. This strong sense of metarepresentation derives, according to the authors, from Perner's reasoning as follows:

> [...] according to Perner, in order for something to be a representation, it must not only be a representation of something, but a representation of something *as being in a certain way*. Hence, in order for something to be a *meta*representation, it must not only be a representation of a representation, but it must be a representation of a representation as being a certain way – namely, as being a representation. (2010: 46)

As we will see in the next section, however, this conclusion is not compelling, since another minimal sense of the notion of metarepresentation can be envisaged.

4. *Meini and Voltolini: a minimally metarepresentational account*

If Meini and Voltolini (2010) agree with Perner's criticisms of the Metarepresentational account sustained by Leslie, they are equally critical of Perner and of the Pernerian accounts illustrated above, according to which pretense would not require any metarepresentational capacity whatsoever. On the contrary, according to Meini and Voltolini pretense necessarily requires a form of metarepresentation, even if only a minimal one. First of all, let us take into consideration their reasons in favor of this minimally metarepresentational approach.

The importance of acknowledging the necessity of a minimal form of metarepresentation in pretense, the authors argue, stems from the need to distinguish the cognitive situation of a pretending subject both from that of a *deluded* subject and from that of a *dissociated* subject (2010: 41ff.). Deluded subjects are those who take some representation of theirs as the representation of an actual state of affairs, when, in fact, this is not the case. A typical example of delusory thought is dreaming: when we dream, we activate a model that we take to be a model of an actual situation, but which represents, instead, a non-actual scenario. In this respect, dreamers can be compared to hallucinating subjects: what they have in common is the fact that they deal only with one representational model, to use Perner's terminology, a model of the actual world, although the representations belonging to this model are not representations of actual states of affairs.[4]

If the cognitive situation of a pretending subject is certainly different from that of a deluded subject, since only the former deals with multiple models, things get more complicated when we consider, for example, those patients who are affected by Capgras syndrome. These subjects recognize a certain person (typically, a close relative or a friend) as identical, in all respects, to some acquaintance of theirs – so, their capacity to recognize friends and relatives is preserved – nevertheless, they sustain that that person is not their relative or friend. For example, a person with Capgras syndrome can recognize that the person in front of him resembles, in all important respects, his wife, and still claim that she is not his wife, but rather an impostor who has taken her place. Analogously to deluded subjects, Capgras patients also mobilize a representational model that they take to be a model of reality (e.g. "that is not my wife"), when, in fact, this is not the case. Still, their situation is more complicated and could be better described as a case of *dissociation*, rather than one of hallucination. In fact, if, on one side, Capgras patients seem to firmly believe that a close relative has been substituted by an impostor, on the other side, they do not express much worry and often behave in a friendly manner towards him or her – a behavior which is at odds, of course, with their beliefs. This is why Young (2000) has supposed that the delirious beliefs of a Capgras patient are not

---

4   True enough, in dreaming, things are not always so neat: on some occasions we do not completely trust what we are dreaming, that is, we have the impression that we are in a world of fantasy. In most cases, however, we take our representations to be representations of actual states of affairs.

integrated into a single belief system, but rather, they are kept separate, as if they belonged to a model different from the model of reality. But if things are so, Meini and Voltolini remark (2010: 41), the cognitive situation of a Capgras patient is dangerously similar to that of a pretending subject, since also in this case the subject is dealing with two different representational models and is capable of keeping them distinct in some way. An even clearer example of dissociation is represented by sleepwalkers. Sleepwalkers typically mobilize two different representational models at the same time: on one side, they certainly possess some imaginary representation – what they are dreaming about – but, on the other side, they must also entertain some perceptual states – those that enable them to move in the space around them, avoiding the obstacles. In this respect, then, their cognitive situation is very close to that of a pretending subject. The only difference seems to be that, even if the sleepwalker is entertaining different representations, belonging to two different models, at the same time she probably ignores which is the real-world model and which the imaginary one. In other words, even if her perceptions of the space around her are quarantined from those of her imaginary world, these representations are not recognized as representations of actual *vs.* non-actual scenarios, and perhaps do not reach the level of consciousness (the sleepwalker's eyes are wide open, but she does not seem to be conscious of what she is seeing).

Now, the authors claim, if one stands with a non-metarepresentational approach like the one sketched by Perner, then one cannot satisfactorily distinguish the case of a dissociated subject like a sleepwalker from that of a pretender. In other words, the definition of a pretending subject as a subject who is capable to deal, at the same time, with two (or more) representational models turns out to be underdetermined and admits also cases which are not genuine cases of pretense. As the authors say:

> The difference between a pretending subject and a dissociated subject lies in the fact that the former *acknowledges* that the representations entertained in the pretend model are not to be lumped together with the representations (s)he simultaneously entertains in the reality model. This is what enables him/her to entertain contradictory representations simultaneously (going back to Leslie's afore-mentioned example, "this is a banana" and "this is not a banana"). It is not only a question of (s)he putting these representations in different representational boxes, as even the dissociated subject does. Unlike the latter, (s)he also *takes* these representations *as* belonging to such distinct boxes. (2010: 42)

But what does it mean, exactly, that the pretender *takes her representations as belonging to different boxes*?

Of course, if this awareness were understood as a fully metarepresentational capacity – a capacity to represent these representations *qua* representations (that belong to different 'boxes' or 'mental spaces') –, then we would be pushed back to Perner's 'strong' notion of a metarepresentation and would have to face all criticisms that have been already moved against Leslie (cf. above, § 2.1). According to the authors, however, this interpretation is not compelling, since there is another, minimal sense in which we can speak of a metarepresentational capacity, a sense which relies, the authors claim, on the distinction between *singular* and *general* thoughts.

More precisely, what the authors propose to do is to apply McDowell's (1982) famous distinction between *singular* and *general* thoughts to second-order thoughts and, in particular, to metarepresentations. So, just as we can distinguish singular first-order thoughts – thoughts having *individuals* as their constituents (for example, the thought: "Hespero is the evening star") – from general first-order thoughts – thoughts that have notions as their constituents (for example, "the star that is the last to disappear in the morning is also the first to appear in the evening") –, much the same way the authors say, we can distinguish between singular second-order thoughts (which contain representations in their content) from general second-order thoughts (which contain, instead, the *notion* of representation in their content).

In other words, according to Meini and Voltolini (2010: 47ff.), we can distinguish between two kinds of metarepresentations: *general* metarepresentations represent representations *qua* representations – i.e. they are about representations and identify representations as representations, thus employing the concept of representation itself; *singular* metarepresentations, on the contrary, are *about* representations without representing them as representations, that is, they contain a representation merely "*qua* instantiation of the relation of representing without being conceived as such".

Now, Meini and Voltolini say, whereas Leslie's account requires – both in its strong and in its weak formulation – *general* metarepresentations, their 'minimally metarepresentational account' requires only *singular* metarepresentations. Both the "Pretense-is-Belief" and the "Pretense-requires-Belief" accounts, in other words, require that the pretender entertains a thought of the kind: "S pretends that *this representation* is F", where the notion of representation is explicitly involved. On the contrary, the authors say, all that is required from the pretending subject is this:

> Pretending subjects have to be aware that their real representations are distinct from their imaginary representations. In order for such an awareness to

have those representations in its content, however, those subjects do not need to conceive these representations as representations. This is by no means surprising. For it is just another case in which one knows that *a* is not *b*, without mobilising the concepts under which *a* and *b* respectively fall. (2010: 48-49)

According to Meini and Voltolini's view, we can thus identify a minimal representational capacity which simply consists of the ability to conceive a certain mental state as separate, or differently located, with respect to other mental states, without recognizing that state as such, that is: as a mental representation of a certain kind. This, the authors claim, is sufficient to distinguish the cognitive situation of a pretender from that of a dissociated subject, precisely because the dissociated subject does not possess this awareness about the 'location' of her own mental states.

Summary of the chapter

In this chapter we have discussed whether and to what extent our capacity for metarepresenting could be involved in pretense. We have examined in detail both the arguments in favor of a Metarepresentational account, like the ones sustained by Leslie and colleagues, and those in favor of a Behavioral account, which nowadays is sustained in particular by Perner (1991), Olson (1993), Suddendorf & Whiten (2001), and Nichols and Stich (2000).

As we have tried to show, both the criticisms moved against a fully Metarepresentational account – especially by Nichols and Stich (2000) – and those raised against the Behavioral account – by Meini and Voltolini (2010) – are quite convincing. We have then taken into consideration the 'minimally metarepresentational' account proposed by Meini and Voltolini and claimed that their position is the best at explaining how we can keep our pretend representations distinct from our genuine ones. Following Meini and Voltolini's proposal, we also claim that what is required by pretense is an only minimal capacity for metarepresenting, that is, a capacity to keep a certain mental content distinct from other mental contents, without the need, however, to recognize this content as a representational content. In chapter 6 we will come back to this point and try to specify how this minimally metarepresentational account can be understood within the relativist framework which our theory relies on.

V.
IMAGINATION IN A RELATIVIST PERSPECTIVE

In the previous chapters I have taken into consideration and analyzed in detail the most important cognitive theories of pretense. In this chapter I will lay the foundations of my own theory, which relies, as previously stated, on the relativist account of our mental states proposed by François Recanati. I will thus start by describing the Strong Moderate Relativist framework delineated by Recanati in his *Perspectival Thought* (2007), and try to specify the nature of a pretend mental state within this framework. What I will try to offer is thus a relativist account of the imagination that I will then apply, in the next chapter, to the specific domain of pretense.

The present chapter is organized in three sections. The first presents the form of relativism proposed by Recanati, that he himself has labeled Strong Moderate Relativism. In the second section I illustrate how this theory has been applied to the mind, providing a fundamental reinterpretation of the mode/content distinction and a solution to some important problems concerning perception, memory and imagination. Finally, in the third section I show that the theory proposed by Recanati implies an architecture of the mind which basically recognizes two main categories of states: egocentric states and anaphoric states, and I try to define the notion of a pretend mental state within this architecture of the mind.

1. *Strong Moderate Relativism*

In his book, *Perspectival Thought*, François Recanati has defended a version of relativism that he has defined as Strong Moderate Relativism, and that he has applied to both language and mind.

According to relativism, the contents of our utterances need not represent all those elements that contribute to the truth-value of the utterances themselves. In other words, if the truth-value of an utterance is determined by two elements, a content and a circumstance of evaluation (this is the principle of *duality*, as Recanati calls it), relativism typically claims that the determinants of the truth-value are distributed over these two components, so that each determinant is "*either* given as an ingredient of content *or* as an aspect of the circumstance of evaluation" (2007: 33-34, this is the principle of *distribution*, according to Recanati's terminology).

A typical example of what distribution consists in is the treatment of tensed sentences given by so-called "temporal relativists". According to Temporal Relativism (cf. e.g. Prior 2003), a tensed sentence like "I baked a cake" would express a temporally-neutral proposition, "I bake a cake" – that can be true at some times and false at others – that falls within the scope of a temporal operator P (the "past operator"), whereas the statement "I will bake a cake" would express the same proposition, "I bake a cake", falling, this time, under the scope of a different operator (the "future operator" F). According to this account, time is thought of as an element which is not part of the explicit content of the utterance – what the utterance *is about* – but which falls, instead, on the side of the circumstance against which the utterance must be evaluated – what the utterance *concerns*.[1]

The idea of distribution, however, is not limited to time. For instance, according to the famous example given by Perry (1986/1993), the content of an utterance "it is raining" is not the complete proposition "it is raining at place *p*", but rather a *propositional function*. That is: a place-neutral proposition that must be *relativized* to a richer circumstance of evaluation, including not only a world, but also a place – the place where it is raining. In this sense, Perry claims, if something is given as part of the situation concerned by an utterance and against which the utterance must be evaluated, it does not have to also be articulated in the content of the utterance itself.

Depending on whether the partial contents that derive from accepting the thesis of distribution are understood as *complete* or *incomplete* contents, two different forms of relativism can be envisaged. According to Radical Relativism, partial contents are *complete*. This form of relativism, Recanati says (2007: 38-39), can be traced back to the Stoics, according to whom a sentence like "Dion is alive" expresses one and the same proposition despite the fact that its truth-value changes at Dion's death. Understood this way, contents are thus temporally neutral but, nevertheless, they are complete.

---

1   Here we are dealing with the famous distinction – delineated by Perry (1986/1993), but adopted also by Recanati – between two different semantic relations: *concerning* and *being about*. Whereas the former defines the relation between a representation and its situation of evaluation, the latter denotes, instead, the relation between a representation and the elements that constitute its content (cf. Recanati 2007: 221).

On the contrary, Moderate Relativism concedes that partial contents are *incomplete*, but postulates that every utterance expresses more than one level of content. More precisely, an utterance such as "Dion is alive" would express both an incomplete content – that Recanati, following the Stoic terminology, labels "*lekton*" – and a complete, truth-conditional content – what Recanati calls the "Austinian proposition". This latter would consist of the two components cited above: the temporally-neutral proposition or *lekton*, depicting Dion as possessing the property of being alive, and the circumstance of evaluation for this content, which also contains a certain time.

The account proposed by Moderate Relativism, Recanati remarks, thus includes two different notions of content: an intuitive notion, that can be traced back to Aristotle and the Stoics, and another, modern notion, that stems from the philosophical reflection of Gottlob Frege. According to the former position, when I think "it is raining" on two different occasions, there is a sense in which I am thinking exactly the same thought; according to the latter, on the contrary, what I am thinking on the two occasions are necessarily two distinct thoughts, since their truth-values can be different (on one occasion I could be right in thinking that it is raining, whereas on another occasion I could be wrong). Moderate Relativism, however, conceives the two notions not as competing but, rather, as complementary. Whereas the former corresponds to the explicit content of a certain sentence – what the sentence *is* really *about* – the Fregean notion specifies the utterance's truth-conditions:

> So 'It is raining' expresses a constant *lekton* whenever and wherever it is used, a content that can be modeled as a function from situations to truth-values or as a set of situations (viz. the set $\{s:$ it is raining in $s\}$); but the complete content of an utterance of 'It is raining' is the Austinian proposition that a certain situation (that which the utterance/thought 'concerns') fits that *lekton*, i.e., belongs to the set of situations in question. (2007: 46)

Still, within Moderate Relativism two different positions can be distinguished, depending on whether the *lekton*, the incomplete content, is thought of as dependent on the context of utterance or not. In the version of Moderate Relativism proposed by Michael Dummett (1985), Recanati observes, this kind of content is clearly context-independent, since it is identical to the content of the sentence-type. On the contrary, Recanati says (2007: 47), according to a different version of Moderate Relativism, e.g. the one proposed by Jon Barwise (cf. Barwise & Etchemendy 1987) and David Kaplan (1989), *lekta* are context-dependent, since they are defined as the contents of sentences *with respect to context*. So, whereas according to Dummett's account a sentence like "It is raining" is expressing the time-relative content that "it is raining at the time of the utterance", in Barwise's and Kaplan's view, the incomplete content expressed by an utterance of "it is raining" is rather that "it is raining at a certain time t" – where time t is determined by the context of utterance.

This latter is also the choice made by Recanati, who thus recognizes the existence of three – rather than only two – levels of content: (1) the meaning of the sentence-type; (2) the *lekton*, which is context-dependent; and (3) the Austinian proposition, the complete, truth-conditional content of the utterance. According to this "three-level version of the two-stage picture", Recanati specifies, the context comes into the picture twice: "first, it provides values for the indexicals, which values contribute to the *lekton*; second, it determines the situation against which the *lekton* is to be evaluated" (2007: 47).

This distinction between three levels of content must also be maintained, according to Recanati, in those cases in which the content of the sentence is not semantically incomplete, i.e. those cases in which the level of the *lekton* coincides with a classical proposition and can thus be thought of as a function from possible worlds to truth values. Even in such cases, in fact, Recanati argues (cf. 2007: 48ff.), we can draw a principled distinction between the content of the sentence (the *lekton*), which is a classical proposition, and the content of the utterance (the Austinian proposition), which, in addition to the proposition, also contains a situation of evaluation. Contrary to the sentence, which simply depicts a certain state of affairs, what the Austinian proposition states, in fact, is that "*the situation in question supports the proposition in question*" (2007: 49). The importance of this difference becomes clear if one considers the following example that Recanati borrows from Barwise and Etchemendy (1987: 29, 121):

> Commenting upon a poker game I am watching, I say: 'Claire has a good hand now'. What I say is true, if Claire has a good hand in the poker game I am watching at the moment of utterance. Suppose I made a mistake and Claire is not among the players in that game. Then my utterance is not true, because the situation it concerns (the poker game I am watching) is not one in which Claire has a good hand at the time of utterance. [...] But suppose that, by coincidence, Claire happens to be playing bridge in some other part of town and has a good hand there. There certainly is a sense in which, in such circumstances, what is said can be considered as 'true' (true by accident, as it were). So we have conflicting intuitions about such a case. Is the utterance true or false? In the SMR framework, we can accept both answers. What is said is true, absolutely speaking, but it is not true *of* the situation the utterance purports to characterize.

[...] If we evaluate the *lekton* abstractly, we get one verdict; if we evaluate the full Austinian proposition, we get another verdict. (2007: 50)

This is precisely what distinguishes Strong Moderate Relativism (from now on, SMR) from a weaker version of it: whereas Weak Moderate Relativism does not distinguish between the *lekton* and the utterance's complete content when the *lekton* is a classical proposition, SMR still maintains that there is a difference between the two and thus is able to explain a case like the one above.

2. Applying SMR to the mind

The SMR account illustrated so far has been applied by Recanati not only to language, but also to the mind. In fact, its application to the mind constitutes one of the main reasons to adopt such an account, according to Recanati, since it allows us to reinterpret the traditional distinction between the mode and the content of a mental state in a way that allows us to solve problems which characterize perception as well as memory and imagination. Let us start by considering the way in which perception can be redescribed in a SMR framework.

2.1. Perception

In applying the SMR theory to the mind, Recanati starts by taking as his main critical target Searle's causal theory of perception, since in Searle (1983; 1991) the conceptual confusion between content and mode – what Recanati labels, after Barwise and Perry (1983), "the fallacy of misplaced information" (2007: 127) – is especially evident. According to Searle, the visual perception of, say, a flower gives rise to a perceptual judgment of the kind "there is a flower there", which is true if and only if:
(1) there is a flower there (this is what Recanati calls the *primary condition*);
(2) the presence of the flower there is what causes my visual experience of a flower (referred to, by Recanati, as the *self-referential condition*).
Now, although Recanati agrees with Searle on the truth-conditions of the state, he disagrees with him on the fact that its propositional content must be identified with these truth-conditions, meaning that the intentional content of this perceptual experience is not simply the proposition that "there is a flower there" but, rather, the conjunctive proposition that "there is a flower

there & there being a flower there is causing this visual experience" (2007: 130). In this case, Recanati observes, the propositional content of the state would be self-referential, since in the second conjunct (the self-referential condition) there is a clear reference to the perceptual experience itself ("my visual experience"). This, Recanati claims, is precisely the fallacy of misplaced information, because something that concerns the perceptual mode is put, on the contrary, in the intentional content of the perception:

> [...] the content of the perception of a flower is the fact that there is a flower there. That fact can be represented in all sorts of modes; for it to be represented in the perceptual mode, it must be the case that the fact itself causes the representation. But this feature, hence the self-referential component whose importance Searle rightly emphasizes, is a property of the perceptual mode of representation, not a property of the content of perceptual representations. (2007: 135)

In other words:

> That the state of affairs represented (there being a flower there) causes the representation of that state of affairs is a condition that has to be met for the representation in question to count as a *perception* (rather than, say, an expectation). It follows that the self-referential condition is determined by the perceptual mode of the state, not by its content. (2007: 131-132)

True enough, Recanati says, the subject who is having a visual experience is typically conscious that she is *perceiving* a flower – rather than, say, *remembering* or *imagining* a flower – so, one can agree that the complete content of her experience is self-referential: her whole experience is not only about the flower, but also about the fact that "there being a flower there is causing her visual experience". The content of the overall experience, however, is to be distinguished from that of the visual experience alone, because it involves much more than the mere content of the visual perception: it also involves the knowledge of the psychological mode that the subject is conscious of.

Now, contrary to the Searlian account, Recanati argues that SMR avoids any possible confusion between these two contents, since it clearly distinguishes the propositional content of a mental state – which is identified with the meaning of the sentence-type[2] – from its truth-conditional content – which consists, instead, in the Austinian proposition (the propositional

---

2   One could wonder why it is the meaning of the sentence-type and not the *lekton* that constitutes the cognitive content of a mental state, thus serving as the object of attitudes in the narrow, psychological sense. The *lekton*, however, must be excluded

content plus the circumstance of evaluation for that content). According to Recanati's account, then, what one explicitly represents when one perceives a flower is simply the fact that "there is a flower there" but, since the role played by this representation is that of a perception and the subject is aware of this fact (he knows that he is perceiving), he also represents this proposition ("there is a flower there") as true "with respect to a very specific situation, namely the subject's *perceptual situation*: a situation which the subject is causally affected by through his senses and which, in particular, causes the occurrence of the mental representation in question" (2007: 135).

2.2. Memory

2.2.1. Conjunctivist vs. metarepresentational analysis

The distinction, proposed by Recanati, between what pertains to the content and what pertains to the mode of a mental state is especially convincing when applied to memory, for it allows us to solve a specific problem concerning our mnestic states. On one hand, our states of memory – more precisely, our episodic memories[3] – seem to share their contents with the perceptual experiences from which they originate: when I remember my previous experience of seeing a flower, I have the impression that the content of my memory is exactly the same as the content of my former visual perception of that flower. On the other hand, however, the remembered content cannot be exactly the same, since in the case of visual perception what I perceive is that "There *is* a flower there", whereas in the case of memory I

---

since, as we have seen, it is *context-dependent* (it incorporates the contextual values of the indexicals) and thus it is not entirely 'in the head' (2007: 115).

3 Recanati appeals to the traditional distinction between *semantic memory* and *episodic memory* (cf. Tulving 1972). Although a precise definition of the two types of memory is quite difficult to give, we can define episodic memory as a first-person memory, which concerns episodes of our life (what is also called a "mental time travel", since we re-experience certain events that happened to us from the same first-person perspective), whereas semantic memory can be defined as a memory for general facts. For example, my belief that "I defended my PhD thesis in Vercelli" is a piece of semantic memory, whereas the way the jury looked, my mood, or the mood I was perceiving around me, etc., are all instances of episodic memory: in all these cases what I retrieve is some information which is encoded in a perceptual (including the proprioceptive) mode, which thus allows me to re-experience what I was experiencing on that day. In his discussion, Recanati focuses only on the latter (cf. 2007: 136).

rather represent to myself the state of affairs: "there *was* a flower there". In other words, whereas in the case of perception the scene which constitutes the intentional content of the state is represented as *present*, in the case of episodic memory the same content is represented as *past* (2007: 137).

A possible solution to this problem could consist of adopting a *conjunctivist analysis* of memory states, like the one considered above in the case of vision. Following Searle, the memory of a flower could be described as a complex experience, composed of two constituents:

(1) the representation that "there is a flower there" (*primary condition*);

(2) the representation of the fact that "this representation ('there is a flower there') causally derives from my former perception of a flower" (*self-referential condition*).

On this account, one could then argue that the similarity between the perception and the memory of a flower depends on the fact that they share the former constituent (the primary condition), whereas their difference depends on the self-referential condition. In other words, memory and perception would be similar but, at same time, different states because their contents are only partially overlapping. This solution, however, does not work, since the primary condition cannot be exactly the same: "in perceiving the flower", Recanati observes, "I judge that there is a flower there. In remembering the flower, I do *not* judge that there is a flower there – only that there was one" (2007: 139). The conjunctivist analysis of memory thus seems to fail at least at explaining how our memories can inherit and reproduce the same propositional content of the perceptual states from which they originated.

One could then opt for a *metarepresentational analysis*, according to which the contents of perception are directly embedded within our mnestic states. In other words, our memories would be states with content: "I had perceptual experience XXX", where "XXX" refers to the content of the perceptual experience itself (e.g. "there is a flower there", 2007: *ibidem*). This solution too, however, brings with it an unwelcome consequence, since according to this account our memories would always be about our former perceptual experiences and would concern the world only in an indirect way. To put it another way: we would always be recalling our perceptual experiences, rather than simply the contents of those experiences.

In this respect, Recanati observes, the conjunctivist analysis is better than the metarepresentational one, since it combines a metarepresentational component (the self-referential condition, that consists of "the subject's consciousness of being in a state which causally derives from a previous perception", 2007: 140) with a direct representation of a state of affairs in the world (the primary condition). As we have seen, however, it seems that the content of this representation cannot be identical to that of the original perceptual state, since in memory it is always accompanied by a 'feeling of pastness' of what is represented.

Now, the problems concerning memory can also be solved, according to Recanati, within the SMR framework. More precisely, analogously to the conjunctivist analysis, SMR also conceives the content of episodic memories as constituted by two components, one that represents a state of affairs in the world and the other a metarepresentational knowledge about that state. Differently from the conjunctivist analysis, however, the problem concerning the feeling of pastness does not arise in the SMR account, since the primary condition is conceived as *neutral with respect to time*, that is, the time is not explicitly represented in the content of the state, but it is only part of the evaluation conditions for that state.

In this sense, the analysis of memory given by Recanati is nothing but the application of the relativist interpretation of tensed sentences to the mind. As we have seen (cf. § 1), in a SMR framework, a sentence like "I saw a flower" is analyzed by distinguishing two levels of content: a temporally-neutral proposition ("I see a flower") – that can be true at some times and false at others – and a complete content (the Austinian proposition), that represents this temporally-neutral proposition as true at a certain time in the past. The same holds for mental contents: in a SMR framework what perception and memory share is a *temporal proposition*, depicting the temporally-neutral fact of "there being a flower there". This content, however, is relativized to different times: in the case of perception, it is thought of as holding in the present situation (the situation in which the representation itself is tokened); in the case of memory, it is thought of as concerning a past situation (the situation in which the perceptual experience was tokened):

> In memory, the same temporally neutral proposition that there is a flower there is presented as true with respect to the situation (and the time) of the *earlier* perceptual experience rather than the situation (and the time) of the *present* memory experience. In the analysis of memory just as in the analysis of perception, the temporal element is carried by the situation of evaluation. (2007: 141)

So, if Recanati distinguishes the content of vision from the content of the overall experience (in which the subject is conscious of their being perceiving, she is conscious of her state as a state of perception) in the case of visual perception, the same happens in the case of memory: the content of a memory is the same content that was previously gained from perception – the primary condition of the two states is exactly the same – but, since I am conscious that I am recalling, I also represent that content (e.g. "there being a flower there") as true relative to a certain past time, rather than to the present time.

Recanati also rules out a possible objection that could be raised against his view. By bringing the time out of the content of the mnestic state, one could argue, the SMR account fails to explain the peculiar phenomenology that characterizes memory, namely, that special feeling of pastness we experience when we remember a certain episode of our life. Since this phenomenology is supposed to derive from the specific content of the state, maintaining that memory and perception share the same (temporally-neutral) content would imply that they should have also the same phenomenological flavor. This conclusion, however, is unwarranted, Recanati claims, because the presupposition on which it relies is unwarranted: there is no reason, in fact, to suppose that the phenomenology of a state must supervene necessarily on the content of the state itself; the mode could equally contribute to its phenomenology, since the mode is something the subject is aware of:

> In the memory mode, the content is presented as true with respect to a past perceptual situation, hence the scene represented is felt as past. In the perception mode, the content is presented as true with respect to the current perceptual situation, hence the scene represented is felt as present. (2007: 142)

On Recanati's account, then, the phenomenology of our mental states would not depend only on their explicit contents but, rather, on the contents of the overall experience, that includes also the subject's awareness of entertaining a certain kind of mental state. In other words, the bearer of a mental state is typically conscious of the state she is in and this consciousness too can contribute to the phenomenology of the state itself.

2.2.2. *Defining episodic memory*

The relativist account endorsed by Recanati is powerful not only because it offers a new and more satisfying account of the contents of memory, but also because it allows us to define in a more accurate way what we call "episodic memory". As said, episodic memory can be described as a first-person memory, a memory for facts directly experienced by the subject, that re-presents these facts as they were experienced before. For example, recalling how I felt the day of my graduation or remembering some episodes from my trip to Russia are instances of episodic memory insofar as I recall these events from a first-person point of view, as if I were experiencing them again. This definition, however, is still too vague. What does it mean, in fact, that episodic memories are memories from the first-person point of view? How, exactly, is this point of view represented in my memories? And what does it mean, in terms of content and mode of the state, that I re-experience certain episodes of my life?

As seen in the previous paragraph, the account of memory that Recanati proposes could be defined as a 'simulationist view', according to which the contents of our episodic memories reproduce exactly the same contents of the perceptions from which they originated, the only difference consisting in the fact that, when I remember, the re-presentation of these contents is accompanied by some form of metarepresentation. More precisely, as we have seen, if I am aware that I am remembering, I not only re-create a certain perceptual content, but I know that that content is to be referred to some time in the past. According to Recanati, however, our states of episodic memory possess another distinctive feature: they are always implicit *de se* thoughts.

De se thoughts, Recanati explains, constitute a subset of the more comprehensive category of *de re* thoughts[4] and, more precisely, they can be conceived as that class of *de re* mental states that concern the bearer of the state. The difference is illustrated by Recanati with the following example (2007: 192):

> Suppose the subject, A, was filmed delivering a speech to an assembly of salesmen. He retained no memory of that experience, but, having recently seen the film, remembers the episode from the film. At this point there are two possibilities: he may have identified himself as the person in the film, or he may not. If he has, this is an 'explicit *de se*' type of case. The thought is *de se*, but subject to error through misidentification. (The subject may have been wrong in identifying himself with the character in the film). If he has not identified himself as the person in the film, this is a *de re* type of case: the subject who remembers the scene in the film remembers himself giving the speech, without realizing it is himself that his memory (and the film) is about.

---

4   On the *de dicto/de re* distinction cf. the classic paper by Quine 1956 and for a presentation of the different interpretations that have been given of this distinction cf. the entry "The De Re/De Dicto Distinction", by Th. McKay and M. Nelson on the *Stanford Encyclopedia of Philosophy*. Here Recanati is employing the distinction in the so-called 'metaphysical sense', according to which a mental state attribution is *de re* with respect to an object *o* just in case it directly attributes a property to *o*. In other words, if I ascribe *de re* to the subject x a certain mental state (e.g. a memory), whose content involves a certain person *a* (who can be x herself), then x stands in the memory relation to a singular proposition that involves *a* as a direct constituent, independently of the specific mode of presentation under which x thinks of *a*.

In one case, then, the subject is entertaining a thought about himself without being aware of the fact that it is himself that his thought is about (he sees a scene from a film in which he appears, but he does not recognize himself in that scene): so his state is *de re* about himself as my perception of a cat is *de re* about that cat, even if I have not recognized that cat as my cat. In the other case, the subject entertains a special kind of *de re* thought – that Recanati calls "*de se*" – since it is a *de re* thought about somebody that the subject has explicitly recognized as himself. More precisely, Recanati calls this kind of state an "explicit *de se* thought", since the subject is explicitly represented in her (perceptual) content.

In addition to this, however, a second kind of *de se* thought can be envisaged: this is "the case in which the subject *has* retained first person memories of the original experience, without the mediation of the film" (2007: *ibidem*). For example, the subject could remember having been at that place, having spoken to the salesmen, he could remember some visages, the feelings he felt, and so on and so forth. In these cases, Recanati says, we are dealing with a different kind of *de se* thoughts, because they are only *implicitly de se*: although these thoughts are first-person, the subject is not explicitly represented in their content. Contrary to the previous case, in which the subject of the thought recognizes himself in the film and thus has an explicit *de se* thought (his thought is about himself in the third-person, as if he could see himself from the outside), in the latter case the subject simply remembers the events and the experiences he had on that occasion, but he is not, himself, explicitly represented in those thoughts.[5]

In the SMR framework, episodic memories are thus defined not only as states that re-present exactly the same contents of previous perceptions, but as states whose contents are *personal propositions*[6]: they do not explicitly represent the bearer of the state, even if they concern the bearer of the state. This peculiarity, Recanati observes, also explains why episodic memories are not subject to *error through misidentification*[7]. In fact, whereas in the

5   This difference can also be explicated by making appeal to the already-mentioned distinction between being about and concerning: whereas an implicit *de se* thought merely *concerns* the bearer of the state, i.e. it has to be evaluated with respect to a situation which contains the bearer of the state, an explicit *de se* thought does not only concern the bearer, but it *is about* the bearer of the state, who is thus articulated in its content.

6   If by 'temporal propositions' we mean temporally-neutral contents, then by 'personal propositions' we mean subject-neutral contents, that is, contents which are neutral with respect to the bearer of the state.

7   Cf. Wittgenstein 1958; Shoemaker 1968; Evans 1982.

case of explicit *de se* thoughts the subject may misidentify the person his thought is about and wrongly believe, for instance, that the subject in question is himself when indeed this is not the case, in the case of implicit *de se* thoughts this error is excluded. As Recanati says (2007: 146):

> If I see that my legs are crossed, I may well misidentify the person whose legs are crossed: what I take to be *my* legs in the mirror may be someone else's. When the belief that my legs are crossed is gained through experiencing my own body from inside, no such mistake is possible.

The same is true of the example above. Whereas I could be wrong in recognizing myself as a certain person that I see in the film, I could not be wrong in thinking that the experiences I am remembering are memories of mine: that is, it could not be the case that my memories are someone else's memories. Contrary to explicit *de se* thoughts, then, implicit *de se* thoughts exhibit what is called *immunity to error through misidentification* (from now on, IEM). Recanati thus reinterprets Evans' claim (1982), according to which "whenever there is IEM, this is evidence that the explicit content of the state does not involve any self-identification on the subject's part", by appealing to the existence of thought whose contents are personal propositions, that is, thoughts whose bearers are not part of the contents of the thoughts themselves.

To sum up, according to the SMR framework endorsed by Recanati, a state of episodic memory is defined not only as a state that represents the same content of some previous perception, but also as a state that implies a double awareness: the awareness of the fact that this content is relative to a previous situation and to some moment in the past (from which arises the characteristic feeling of pastness), and the awareness of the fact that this content is relative to me, to the bearer of the state (from which emerges, Recanati says, the *sense of ownership* of our mental states).

2.3. Imagination

2.3.1. Imagining de dicto *and* de re

The distinction we have just pointed out, between implicit and explicit *de se* thought, can also be found in the case of imagination. Recanati (2007: 195-196) cites the famous example given by Vendler (1979: 161), in which, while looking from a cliff at some people swimming in the ocean, one man asks another: "Imagine swimming in the water". As stressed by Vendler, the subject's imaginative activity can take two forms. In one case the subject can imagine being in the ocean, i.e. being shaken by the waves, feeling the coldness of the water, tasting its saltiness, and so on: these are, according to Vendler, instances of *subjective imagination*. In the other case, on the contrary, the subject can imagine seeing himself swimming in the ocean, as if he could look at himself from above the cliff: this case is an instance of what Vendler defines as *objective imagination*.

Now, these two different forms of imagination clearly resemble the two different cases of memory illustrated above: the case in which I simply remember having given a speech to the salesmen (an instance of episodic memory) and the case in which I remember having seen myself in a film in which I was giving a speech to the salesmen. Analogously to memory, the difference between subjective and objective imagination can also be interpreted, Recanati observes, as a difference between implicit and explicit *de se* imaginings: whereas in the first case we are clearly dealing with some implicit *de se* thoughts – the imaginings concern the subject's experience, but the subject is not part of the content of that experience – in the second case the subject has some explicit *de se* thoughts, since she herself is part of the content of the states that she is entertaining at that moment (207: 196).

Still, Recanati observes, the case of imagination seems to pose a special problem. More precisely, it would seem that all imaginings are necessarily *de dicto*. Contrary to perception and memory, whose contents are determined by external factors such as the identity of the objects that stand in the right causal-epistemic relation to us, the contents of imagination seem to be determined by what Recanati calls, after Williams (1973), an "imaginative project" (2007: 196). For example, when I imagine seeing myself in the water, what I do is to explicitly stipulate that the object of my imagination – that person in the water – is me (2007: 199). As a consequence – and contrary to memory – it seems that I can never be wrong about what I am imagining: it is not possible, in other words, that I imagine myself in the water and that it turns out that it is not myself I am imagining about. According to this view, then, *de re* thoughts – and thus also the sub-class of *de se* thoughts – would seem to be impossible in the case of imagination. This conclusion, however, is not compelling, as Recanati shows with the following example.

Suppose I am told that a member of my university has gained a considerable grant. I may come to believe something about *that lucky fellow* (e.g. that "it would be good if *that lucky fellow* now bought some books for the library"): in this case, I would entertain a *de re* belief about him or her. But, if it turned out that, unbeknownst to me, that lucky fellow were me, then I would have entertained a *de re* thought about myself (that is, a *de se* thought). So, Recanati observes, a *de re* thought can be obtained also in this 'derivative manner', since one representation demonstratively refers to the intentional object of another representation – in this case, the intentional object of the representation entertained by the person who gave me this information (2007: 197).

Now, the same can be true of the imagination. I could in fact not only believe something about that lucky fellow, but I may also imagine something about him or her – for example, I may imagine that she or he will be the next dean of the University. In this case, my imagining would also be about *that lucky fellow* – the fellow who is explicitly represented in someone else's mind and whose identity is determined by some external factors that I ignore. So our imaginings can also inherit a *de re* character, even if only in the *intermodal* cases, i.e. in those cases in which they are *anaphorically linked* to some other *type* of state. An imaginative state, in other words, can derive its *de re* character from a belief – as in the case cited above – but not from another imagining. As Recanati says, I may imagine

> that a member of my university becomes the next president of the US, and keep fantasizing about that imaginary character. Even if I happen to have all the properties I imagine that person to have (being a member of this university, being the next president of the US, etc.), imagining that person to be *F* would still not be a case of unwittingly imagining *myself* to be *F*. (2007: 198)

According to Recanati, even if *de re* cases are harder to get in the imaginative mode than in the memory mode, their possibility cannot be excluded *a priori*: my imaginings can have a *de re* character, although this character can be inherited only from a belief or another non-imaginative state of mine.

2.3.2. *Imagining* de se *and* quasi-de se

Recognizing that some of our imaginings can also be *de re*, and, in particular, that we can also have implicitly *de se* thoughts in the case of the imagination, Recanati observes, allows us to solve a further problem, concerning some special cases of imagination which seem to imply a *metaphysical impossibility*. A typical example consists in imagining being someone else, for example imagining being Napoleon. Since I am an individual different from Napoleon and my identity is not among my accidental properties, this case seems to be *prima facie* impossible: "I might have been a high-ranking general, or an emperor. But it is not the case that

I might have been Napoleon himself", says Recanati (2007: 203), "still, I can easily *imagine* being Napoleon".

The problem, Recanati argues, is created by the presence of the self within the content of this imagining: if the self is part of the content of my thought, then I cannot literally imagine that "*I, myself*, am *Napoleon*". Of course, I could imagine myself at the battle of Waterloo – that is, I could imagine *seeing myself* involved in that battle (an instance of objective imagination) – but this would not amount to imagine being Napoleon; rather, it would amount, at best, to imagine myself in a situation analogous to that in which Napoleon was involved (cf. Vendler 1979: 172-173). When I say that "I imagine being Napoleon", Recanati observes, what I have in mind is some kind of first-person imagining (or subjective imagining, to use Vendler's terminology), a reproduction of the experiences that Napoleon must have undergone at a certain moment in his life (for example, during the battle of Waterloo).

Now, this kind of imagining, Recanati claims, can be explained only by appealing to the existence of implicit *de se* thoughts: thoughts whose contents do not contain the bearer of the thought itself as a constituent, but that simply represent the properties which one self-ascribes (2007: 203-204). This means that, when I imagine being Napoleon, the content of my imagining is not that "*I* am Napoleon", but rather, what I represent is simply "being Napoleon". For example, if I imagine being Napoleon at the battle of Waterloo, I will imagine what Napoleon could have felt on that occasion, his fear, his excitement, his effort in the fighting, the enemies he was facing, etc: "imagining being Napoleon" thus means precisely to rehearse these states in me (the fear, the excitement, his possible beliefs and desires, etc.), and then to attribute them to Napoleon.

In this sense, then, analogously to both perception and memory, a case of imagination can also be constructed as a state which involves two levels of content:

(1) the representation of a personal proposition, e.g. "being excited" (this is the narrow content of the imagining);

(2) the representation of the fact that this representation concerns Napoleon (this is the complete content of the overall experience, corresponding to what we have called the "Austinian proposition").

Against this account, however, one could move the following objection. If the contents of our *de se* imaginings are identified with personal propositions, one could argue, then the problem – the metaphysical impossibility – does not disappear, but it is only pushed to the next step: that is, the problem no longer figures in the narrow content of the imagining, but it figures in the complete content of the overall experience. In other words, when I imagine being Napoleon, what I do is simply to imagine certain personal propositions ("being excited", "feeling fear", "waiting for the battle", etc.), and then I *pretend* to ascribe to myself-Napoleon these propositions but, again, I am not really Napoleon, so either I ascribe these properties to me or to Napoleon.

According to Recanati, however, this objection arises only if we fail to recognize that it is not the imaginer to whom certain properties must be ascribed but, rather, it is Napoleon himself. In other words,

> when I imagine being Napoleon and fighting the battle of Waterloo, I imagine certain properties being instantiated, but – in central cases at least – it is not to myself that I (self-)ascribe the properties in question. Rather, I ascribe them to *Napoleon*. (2007: 204)

What Recanati is suggesting is that, when I imagine being another individual:

(1) I do not imagine *me* being another individual but, rather, I imagine some of the properties that she/he did/does instantiate. For example, if I imagine being Napoleon, I can imagine fighting on Waterloo's battlefield, being crowned by the Pope, etc.: none of these states contains the subject as part of their content;

(2) moreover, none of these properties is ascribed to the bearer of the state, but rather, they are ascribed to another individual and relativized to her/his situation. As Recanati observes (2007: 206),

> on this view, not only I am not a constituent of the state of affairs which is the content of my imagination, but even if we look at the complete content (the 'Austinian' proposition), including the situation in which the imagined state of affairs is imagined to hold, I – the actual imaginer – do not come into the picture. The content of the imagination is assumed to hold in *Napoleon's* situation.

In this sense, Recanati says, the state entertained by the subject is not precisely a *de se* thought but, rather, a *quasi*-de se *thought* because, even if it is first-person, the bearer of the state is contained neither in the (narrow) content nor in the situation of evaluation concerned by that state (represented in the content of the overall experience).

This peculiarity also draws a difference between perception and memory on one hand, and imagination on the other hand. As we have seen before (§ 2.2), memory differs from perception in the fact that, while the contents of perception can only concern the time at which the representation is tokened, the contents of memory must be relativized to the past and, more precisely, to a time previous to the time of their tokening. Memory, however, can be paired with perception due to the fact that the subject to whom its contents are relativized must necessarily be the bearer of the state: in this sense, Recanati says, although perhaps possible in other words, states of *quasi-perception* and *quasi-memory* do not exist in the actual world (cf. 2007: ch. 21). On the contrary, imagination is such that the subject concerned by the imagining need not to be the bearer of the state, but can be every subject who is presently the focus of the imaginer: when I imagine being Napoleon at the battle of Waterloo, I not only rehearse certain properties of persons, but I also think that these properties are relative to a situation in which the bearer of these properties is not me, but Napoleon himself.

This feature, Recanati remarks, is not peculiar to imagination alone, but also characterizes some 'non-imaginative' states. An example is empathy: when I empathize with someone, what I do is to feel what the other person is feeling – so, again, I reproduce an emotional reaction, and thus a property of an individual – but I attribute this feeling not to myself, but to somebody else, i.e. I relativize this property to the situation experienced by another person and not by myself (2007: 210).

Not all mental states, then, concern the *hic et nunc* situation – the situation in which the state itself is tokened – but some – as our imaginings – may concern any situation the subject is currently focusing on, be it the situation in which the representation itself is tokened or not.

3. *Beyond egocentricity*

As we have seen in the previous section, states of imagination can certainly share the same content with states of genuine perception, or with memories. For example, I can feel excited as a consequence of being in a certain situation, but I can also imagine that someone else is excited: this means rehearsing the same kind of state (a state of excitation), but relativizing this state to another person and another situation (for example, as seen above, it can be Napoleon before Waterloo's battle). Or, to take a case of memory, I can remember how the view from the window of my hotel in Siena was yesterday: this means I am able to reproduce a state with the same visual content as my previous perception, but I relativize this content to a situation, and especially to a time (i.e. yesterday morning) different from the situation and time at which I am reproducing this perceptual content. The question, however, is to understand what it means, from the cognitive point of view, to *relativize* a certain state of mind to a certain situation, different from the one the subject is presently in. This is explained by Recanati by appealing, precisely, to the anaphoric mode.

3.1. *Against egocentricity*

The anaphoric mode is introduced by Recanati in opposition to Lewis's (1978/1983) treatment of our mental states. According to Lewis, Recanati says:

> Whenever a representation is tokened in the subject's mind, the content of the representation is evaluated with respect to a situation involving the subject and the time and place of the tokening. In other words, the content is construed as a property which is ascribed to the context in which the representation is tokened. If the subject feels that she is hot, the content of the representation is the property of being hot, which the subject ascribes to herself at the present time. If the subject believes that this is a hot saucer, the content of the representation is another property which the subject ascribes to herself at the present time, namely the property of being R_{dem}-related to an x such that x is a hot saucer. If the subject conjectures that it was hot two weeks ago, she conjecturally ascribes to the context she is in the property of being two weeks later than a situation in which it was hot at the same place. (2007: 269-270)

Lewis's position is thus presented by Recanati as a typical *egocentric theory*, that is, a theory according to which every thought we can entertain always concerns the *hic et nunc* situation (the context of its tokening). Even states such as conjectures, memories or imaginings would concern, by this account, the situation in which they are tokened, rather than a different one. For example, remembering that an event x happened yesterday would mean to ascribe to the context that I am presently in, the property of being one day later than the situation in which x happened.

This position, Recanati observes, leads to a problem, since entertaining a memory would thus necessarily mean to be able to specify "the relation R to which the subject stands to the state of affairs remembered" (2007: 272). In other words, if remembering how cold it was in Chicago exactly one year ago means nothing but ascribing to the context I am currently in the property of "being exactly one year later than a situation in which I was freezing in Chicago", the relation R that I entertained with a certain content is necessarily internalized and becomes an aspect of the content of my actual thought, which would thus express not only a relativized proposition that *p*, but a proposition of the kind: "In *my* past experience (the situation I was in one year ago), it was the case that p ('I was freezing')". But, Recanati rightly observes (2007: 273), the subject who remembers or imagines need not be aware of the contextual relation R which she has with the object of her thought, nor must she be able to articulate it. This is why, according to Recanati, Lewis's account is to be rejected: it requires too much from the subject, because it requires that, when the subject is holding a certain type of state (e.g. a belief, or a memory), she must be able to specify the relation holding between herself and the content of her state.

What Recanati proposes is to consider the possibility that our mental contents can be entertained, instead, in two different modes: the egocentric and the anaphoric mode. More precisely, egocentric states would be those states that we entertain without representing, at the same time, the situation concerned by them nor – as sustained by Lewis – the relation we entertain towards them; anaphoric states would be instead all those states in which we represent not only a certain content, but also the situation concerned by that content without, however, explicitly representing the relation R that we entertain towards that content. As we will see in detail in the next section, this is in fact true of all states that are different from perception: in this sense, then, contrary to Lewis's theory, egocentric states can be understood as those special cases in which the representation of a certain content is not accompanied by the representation of the situation concerned by that content. Neither egocentric nor anaphoric states, however, imply the explicit representation of the relation holding between the bearer of the state and the state itself. Let us now consider in deeper detail how Recanati conceives these two main modes of presentation.

3.2. *The anaphoric mode*

In order to understand the way in which Recanati conceives the distinction between egocentric and anaphoric modes of presentation, we must start by taking into consideration the criticism that Recanati moves against John Perry's famous theory of unarticulated constituents. In his *Thought without Representation*, Perry considers the following case (1986/1993: 211):

> Suppose […] that my son has just talked to my older son in Murdock on the telephone, and is responding to my question, "How are things there?". Then his remark ["It is raining"] would not be about Palo Alto [the place where he is], but about Murdock [...]. My son's belief [is] about Murdock, and his intention [is] to induce a belief in me that [is] about Murdock by saying something about

Murdock. Here it is natural to think that we are explaining which unarticulated constituent a statement is about, in terms of something like the *articulated* constituents of the beliefs and intentions it expresses.

According to Perry, the content of an utterance like "it is raining" can contain some unarticulated constituent, that is, a constituent which is not explicitly represented by a term in the utterance (in the case above, this constituent is the place at which it is raining). This depends on the fact that this constituent, although not articulated in the utterance, is instead explicitly articulated in the speaker's mind. In other words, when Perry's son says to his father that "it is raining", what he is thinking, according to Perry, is not merely that "it is raining", but that "it is raining *in Murdock*": his thought *is about* Murdock and does not merely *concern* that place. As a consequence, Perry claims, also the utterance which expresses his thought *is about* Murdock, although this constituent is not explicitly articulated in it. To put it another way, in Perry's view, when I think a thought like "It is raining", I am always thinking also about the place at which it is raining, that is, I am necessarily thinking "it is raining in Palo Alto", or "it is raining in Murdock", etc. The only cases in which this is not true are those in which it is impossible that the content of my state concerns a situation different from the *hic et nunc*:

> In those parts of our life where there is an external guarantee that the weather information we receive and our actions will concern our own locale, there is no reason for our beliefs to play the internal coordinating role they need to at other times. (1986/1993: 216)

According to Perry, then, the only cases in which I simply think "it is raining" are my perceptions, that is, those states whose contents necessarily concern the situation in which the state itself is tokened. In other words, if a state is a state of perception, then its content necessarily concerns the situation that the bearer of the state is presently in. In all other cases, on the contrary, it never happens that I simply think a content like "it is raining", but what I think is instead "it is raining at place *a*", because in these cases the situation concerned by the state is not determined by the external environment, but rather it depends on the beliefs entertained by the subject. If I look out of the window and perceive that "it is raining", the fact that my thought concerns the place at which the thought itself is tokened is a direct consequence of the fact that it is raining and that I am perceiving that it is raining. If I am in Palo Alto, while the sun is shining, but I think about the weather in Murdock, the fact that my thought "it is raining" concerns

Murdock, rather than Palo Alto, depends instead on the fact that this place is explicitly articulated in my thought, that is, due to the fact that I am thinking of Murdock, and not of Palo Alto.

Now, whereas Recanati agrees with Perry on the existence of these two different cognitive situations, he does not agree with Perry's treatment of those cases in which the state does not concern the situation of its tokening. According to Recanati, when I think "it is raining" but my representation does not concern the *hic et nunc* situation, it is not necessary that I think: "It is raining at place *a*". In some cases, he argues, I could be simply representing the fact that "it is raining", whereas the situation concerned by my state could be represented in some other thought of mine, to which my state "it is raining" is *anaphorically linked*. In other words, although Recanati agrees with the idea that there are some unarticulated constituents of utterances that can be articulated in the corresponding mental representations entertained by the subject, what he claims is that there is no need to postulate that these constituents must necessarily be articulated in one and the same representation:

> The fact that Perry's son must think of Murdock and intend to say something about Murdock when he utters "It is raining" possibly entails that Murdock is articulated in some mental representation of his, but does *not* entail that the belief he expresses by his utterance "It is raining" is the locus of that articulation. [...] I grant that the relevant place (Murdock) is articulated in some mental representation in the speaker's mind, which mental representation crucially serves as background for his utterance "It is raining", but I deny that the mental representation in question must be identical to the very belief he expresses by this utterance. (2007: 226)

Suppose that I am in Palo Alto, the sun is shining and it is very hot, but nevertheless I want to imagine that it is a rainy day. I thus imagine how the things around me would look on a rainy day: I imagine that we are in the middle of a heavy shower, with a strong wind that is producing a loud noise, etc. All these instances of visual and acoustic imagery concern an imaginary situation, one in which it is raining in Palo Alto, but this does not mean that I have to represent the fact that "it is raining *in Palo Alto*". Rather, what I represent is the fact that "it is raining heavily", that "there is a noise created by the wind", that "my neighbor's tree is bent by the wind", etc. Of all these facts, however, I am conscious that they are relative to Palo Alto, since Palo Alto is presently the attentional focus of my thoughts. In other words, since my "imaginative project" concerns a day of rain in Palo Alto, all the instances of imagery that I create concern Palo Alto, the place that is *cognitively salient* to my mind at this moment[8]. The same is true in the case of Perry's son: even if he is in Palo Alto and the sun is shining, the situation cognitively salient in his mind is Murdock, the place where his brother is, and it is relative to that situation that he is presently entertaining the thought "it is raining".

This is precisely what Recanati means by the "anaphoric mode of presentation": when a representation is entertained in the anaphoric mode, this representation never comes alone, so to say, but the subject is able to relate the content of this representation to a certain situation, which is the attentional focus of the subject at that moment:

> Our thoughts [...] may concern whatever entity is currently salient in our mind, even though the entity in question is not articulated in the thought that concerns it, but only in some other mental representation that serves as cognitive background for it. To accept this relation between thoughts, where one thought serves as background for another and determines what the other concerns, is to accept the existence of a mode characterized by the parameter: *thing currently being talked or thought about*. This mode, whether in discourse or thought, we may call the 'anaphoric mode'. [...] in the anaphoric mode one does 'as if' something was given in the context, while it is given only mentally or discursively. (2007: 284)

Before carrying on, I want to stress the difference between the solution given by Recanati and the one given by Lewis. As previously stated, the problem with Lewis's 'egocentric theory' is that it implies that the bearer of a state must always be conscious of the cognitive relation she entertains with that state, and this, as we have seen (cf. § 3.1), does not seem to necessarily be the case. This problem, however, does not affect Recanati's conception of our mental states. In particular, when Recanati says that anaphoric representations imply that their bearers are able *to relate* a certain content to a certain situation, which is their attentional focus at a given moment, what he means is only that the bearer of an anaphoric state is always aware of the fact that a certain mental content concerns a certain situation (e.g. a certain world, a certain space, a certain time, etc.), but this is not to say that she is aware of the relation (the mental attitude) that she entertains together with that content. For example, if I am imagining a certain content, I am simply aware of the fact that that content (e.g. the content that "it is raining") concerns an

---

8   In cognitive linguistics the notion of cognitive saliency is employed to mean "the activation of concepts in actual speech events", in the sense that these concepts would be "loaded [...] into current working memory and thus become part of a person's center of attention" (Schmid 2007: 119-120).

imaginary situation (i.e. a situation which does not hold in the actual world), but this does not mean that I am aware of the mental attitude (imagination) that I entertain towards that content.

3.3. *Cognitive significance*

The introduction of the anaphoric mode also helps Recanati to avoid a possible problem with his theory: namely, the problem of explaining the different cognitive significance that two instances of the same thought can have in two different individuals, or in the same individual on two different occasions (cf. 2007: 286-287).

A typical example posing this kind of problem is the situation that has been discussed above, in which both of Perry's sons – the one who lives in Palo Alto and the other, who lives in Murdock – apparently think exactly the same thing ("It is raining"). Even if the two brothers are thinking the same thing at the same time, their behaviors are different: whereas the brother in Murdock, after having looked out of the window and thought "it is raining", takes the umbrella before going out, cancels his plans for a picnic, etc., the brother in Palo Alto does not exhibit any of these behaviors. So, the problem is: if the two brothers share the same belief, how can we explain the fact that the dispositions to act associated with it are indeed different? What should we appeal to in order to explain this difference?

Note that, on Perry's account, this problem does not exist, because the thoughts of his sons are different. More precisely, whereas the son in Murdock is entertaining a thought concerning the local weather ("It is raining"), his brother in Palo Alto is entertaining a thought concerning a place different from the place where he presently is ("It is raining in Murdoch"). So, although the two brothers say the same thing – "It is raining" – the thoughts they entertain differ in their contents: whereas the brother in Murdock is simply representing the fact that "it is raining", the brother in Palo Alto is thinking about the fact that "it is raining *in Murdock*" and this difference could perhaps determine a difference in their behaviors.

According to Recanati, on the contrary, the thoughts entertained by the two brothers can be perfectly identical: they both could be thinking nothing but the relativized proposition that "it is raining" and, moreover, their thoughts could both concern the same situation, that is, they could both concern the weather in Murdock (2007: 287). The difference in the cognitive significance of the two thoughts is explained, on his account, by appealing not to the contents, but rather, to the *modes* in which these thoughts are entertained. In other words, whereas in the case of the brother living in

Murdock the thought "it is raining", being a perceptual judgment, is enter-tained in the egocentric mode, in the case of the brother living in Palo Alto the same thought is entertained in the anaphoric mode this is because it concerns a situation different from the situation in which the subject pres-ently is and, Recanati goes on, contrary to the representations entertained in the egocentric mode, those entertained in the anaphoric mode are such that "the dispositions to act [...] are *inhibited*" (2007: *ibidem*).

The difference in the way our cognitive systems treat two representations endowed with the same content, Recanati thus concludes, can be explained as a difference in the mode in which the content is entertained: our cogni-tive systems, in other words, could be sensitive not only to the content of a given representation, but also to the links that this representation possibly has with other states, or, likewise, to the fact that this representation is ac-companied by some other representation, the representation of the situation concerned by the content of the former state.

3.4. *The nature of a pretend mental state*

To sum up, according to Recanati we can divide our mental states into two main groups: egocentric states – those states which necessarily con-cern the situation in which they are tokened – and the anaphoric states – those states which concern a situation different from that in which they are tokened. Moreover, as already stated, anaphoric states, rather than being the exception, are instead the norm in the sense that, apart from our percep-tions, all other states – imaginings, memories, desires, etc. – are given in the anaphoric mode.

One could then raise the following question: if memories, imaginings, conjectures, etc., are all states in the anaphoric mode, how can we distin-guish one type of state from the others? For example, in what ways would an imagining differ from a memory state? And how, exactly, should we characterize a *pretend mental state* – that is, the kind of imagining which is employed in our games of make-believe?

Now, if we follow Recanati's account, it is clear that different kinds of anaphoric states can be distinguished on the basis of the type of situ-ation to which they are anaphorically linked. For example, in the case of memory, the situation concerned by the content of this state is always a situation previous to the *hic et nunc* situation: when I remember a certain event of my life, the representation of this event is anaphorically linked to the representation of a situation which belongs to the actual world, but to a different time. For example, if I remember how the mountains looked yesterday morning, I not only visualize the mountains, but I am conscious, at the same time, that this representation concerns yesterday morning. To put it in another way, a state of memory is necessarily anaphoric for the aspect of time, since the time concerned by our memories is *necessarily different* – and, more precisely, anterior – to the time at which a memory is tokened. On the contrary, and with the same necessity, the subject of the situation must coincide with the subject who is presently holding the representation (because, as we have seen, it cannot be the case that I am remembering someone else's memories), and the same is true for the world of evaluation: the world to which I relativize my memories can only be the actual world, because it is the only world that I actually experienced.

Things are different in the case of imagination. For example, when I imagine eating a chocolate cake, I can entertain different kinds of imaginings: motor imaginings (representing my mouth's movement) or gustatory imaginings (I can imagine the taste of the chocolate), but these representations are always accompanied by some other mental state, which specifies the situation concerned by them; this representation, to which my imaginings are anaphorically linked, typically represents a world different from the actual one. This representation can also specify something more: for example, it can represent the time – if the time is different from the time of the tokening – or it can represent another subject – if, as in the case of Napoleon, the subject is different from the bearer of the state – and so on. In this sense, then, a state of imagination is more 'free' than a memory, because, contrary to a memory, the subject and the time (and other aspects as well) are also concerned by an imagining and do not need to coincide with the subject and the time of the context in which the imagining is tokened. One could argue that the distinctive feature of the imagination consists of the fact that the world to which the imagining is relativized is always a non-actual world: in imagination, one could claim, what is explicitly represented is always thought of as concerning a possible world, distinct from the actual one. This, however, even if true in the majority of cases, is not true for every case of imagination.

The case considered above (cf. § 2.3.2) – the case in which I imagine being Napoleon – is a good counterexample, that is, a case for which this constraint does not hold. Contrary to the cases in which I imagine being a princess, or being Anna Karenina, when I imagine being Napoleon, it seems that the world concerned by the personal properties that I instantiate (e.g. the fact of being excited for the imminent battle, the fact of being proud to lead the French army, etc.) is precisely the actual world: my representations concern the world where I find myself, although they concern a time anterior to the present time and a subject different from the bearer of the state. To put it differently, when I imagine being Napoleon, what I do is to re-instantiate some properties that I suppose were *actually* instantiated by another individual – Napoleon – at a certain moment in the past. In this sense, in imagining being Napoleon, what I am doing is nothing but an exercise in (third person) *mindreading*. The only unusual aspect is the fact that the personal proposition I recreate is thought of as concerning a past situation, rather than a present one, that is: it does not concern a contemporary, as usually happens in mindreading, but someone who lived in another epoch.

To sum up, in a SMR account an imagining, or what we have called a "pretend mental state", can be described as the kind of state that can be anaphoric for every aspect of the situation of evaluation, that is, the kind of state whose situation of evaluation can differ from the *hic et nunc* for any aspect whatsoever.

Summary of the chapter

The goal of this chapter has been to outline the relativist framework on which my theory of pretense relies. I have thus tried to illustrate how a pretend mental state must be conceived within a relativist account of our mental states, such as that proposed by François Recanati. This has led me to adopt an architecture of the mind which envisages two main types of mental states: egocentric states and anaphoric states.

In particular, Recanati considers the anaphoric mode of presentation as the mental mode that makes *simulation* possible. More precisely, the anaphoric mode can be described as the mode which is at the basis of the *imaginative displacement* that characterizes simulation, Recanati says, borrowing Bühler's terminology:

> […] in the anaphoric mode, we treat a remote situation which has been evoked *as if* it was egocentrically given. Talking about a situation indeed makes it 'present to the mind' in such a way that it can serve as a substitute for the egocentric situation and give rise to 'imagination-oriented deixis'. (2007: 286)

In the next and last chapter I will try to clarify how this relativist account of the imagination can be applied to the domain of pretense, and which advantages this account offers in comparison to the other accounts we have considered in the course of this book.

VI.
A RELATIVIST ACCOUNT OF PRETENSE

In the previous chapter I have sketched a theory of the imagination based on the (strong moderate version of) relativism proposed by François Recanati (2007). In particular, I have tried to specify how a pretend mental state could be understood within this framework and distinguished from other kinds of mental states. In this chapter I will discuss in detail the theory of pretense that can be built upon the SMR framework and, most importantly, the kind of advantages that this theory can offer, if compared to the other accounts considered so far.

As seen, accepting the SMR account means accepting a fundamental distinction between two kinds of mental states: egocentric states – states which are 'self-standing' – and anaphoric states – states which are anaphorically linked to some other mental states, which appear to be cognitively relevant at a given moment. Pretend mental states belong, as previously stated, to this latter category, so they require that the subject is able to relativize their content to some other information which is cognitively relevant in the pretender's mind.

The first step towards a full-blown relativist account of pretense will thus consist of specifying what it means, exactly, to 'relativize' a mental state to some other mental state, and to determine to what extent this capacity for 'relativizing contents' depends on our metarepresentational abilities. In the first section of this chapter I will thus commence by taking into consideration the kinds of abilities that, according to Recanati (2000), are required in order to engage in pretense (§ 1.1). I will show that the metarepresentational abilities that Recanati attributes to 2 and 3 year olds are too demanding for such young children, but I will also show that the his relativist account is compatible with an only minimally-metarepresentational account such as the one proposed by Meini and Voltolini (2010). I will thus claim that the notion of relativization can be satisfactorily accounted for by adopting this latter theory (§ 1.2).

In the second section I will start by describing some typical examples of pretense from the relativist point of view that I endorse (§ 2.1) and I will then try to show that a relativist account of our mental states best explains some crucial features of pretense, such as the cognitive quarantine of our mental states or the fundamental phenomenon of anchoring (§ 2.2). I will conclude with some more general remarks on the relationship between imagination, pretense and mindreading in a relativist account of our mental states (§ 3).

1. *Metarepresentational abilities*

As we have seen in the previous chapter (cf. §§ 3.1-3.2), Recanati criticizes Lewis's proposal to treat our mental states as properties of the context of their tokening, because this theory implies that the subject should be aware of the relation that she entertains with the contents of her mental states. On the contrary, as we have seen, Recanati proposes a distinction between two main classes of mental states: egocentric and anaphoric states, whose difference seems to consist in the fact that only the latter requires from their bearer that she represents not only a certain content, but also the situation concerned by that content.

One could however object that Recanati makes a mistake analogous to that made by Lewis, since it seems that when a subject is remembering something, or is imagining something, she must be able to represent a certain content as relative to a certain situation (the situation of evaluation for that content), and thus, she must be aware of what a situation of evaluation is. In other words, if Lewis's account implied that the subject must be aware of the relation she entertains to a certain content (she must be aware that she is imaginatively related, or demonstratively related – in the case of perception – to a certain content), Recanati's theory would imply that the bearer of an anaphoric state must be aware of the fact that she is representing not only a certain mental content, but also the situation of evaluation of that given state. This conclusion, however, is not compelling: all an SMR account requires from the bearer of an anaphoric state is that she is aware of the fact that a certain mental content is relative to a certain situation cognitively relevant to her mind. For example, she must be conscious of the fact that a certain possible content is relative to a fictional situation, to a past situation, or even to a future, possible situation, without conceptualizing this situation as a situation of evaluation.

Most importantly, one could ask, what does it mean, exactly, that the subject is able to 'relativize' a certain representational content to some other state? Recanati does not say much on this point. If we interpret this capacity as a metarepresentational ability, and we stay with the account of pretense play that he gives in *Oratio Obliqua, Oratio Recta* (2000), however, the SMR framework has to face some important objections, since Recanati's account of pretense play requires too strong a metarepresentational capacity, that children would hardly possess before the age of 4. As I will argue, however, an SMR account of our pretend mental states is not committed to the metarepresentational abilities sketched in *Oratio Obliqua*, but it is also compatible with an only minimally metarepresentational theory, like the one proposed by Meini and Voltolini (2010). Let us start by considering the strong metarepresentational account of pretense given by Recanati (2000).

1.1. *A strong metarepresentationalist account*

In *Oratio Obliqua, Oratio Recta* Recanati distinguishes two main ways of thinking about a certain situation. On one hand, we can think something *about* a certain situation, as when we think that "it is raining at location *l*"; on the other hand, we can think something *with respect to* a situation, so that the location *l* simply constitutes the situation concerned by our thought, but it is not part of the content of the thought itself. In other words, either we think that a certain fact holds in a certain situation (as when we think "it is raining *in Paris*"), and thus we explicitly represent the situation in which that fact holds, or we only represent a certain state of affairs ("It is raining"), whereas the situation concerned by the state is only part of our background knowledge. So far nothing new: we are dealing with the afore-mentioned distinction between the two semantic relations of *being about* and *concerning* (cf. V.1). Recanati, however, also distinguishes two main cognitive processes that he labels, respectively, *reflection* and *projection*.

What we do during *reflection*, according to Recanati, is take into consideration a certain situation *qua* situation, that is, from thinking something *with respect to* a certain situation ("It is raining"), we come to think something *about* a certain situation ("It is raining in Paris"), thus making that situation part of the explicit content of our thought. This change in the content, Recanati remarks, also implies a change in the situation concerned by the representation. For example, if, when I think "it is raining," the concerned situation is Paris, when I think "it is raining in Paris", the concerned situation is a wider one, because, typically, my intention is to contrast Paris with some other place, e.g. with some other European capital, where instead the sun is shining (2000: 65-66).

Projection just consists of the inverse process: from thinking *about* a certain situation, we come to think something *with respect to* a certain situation. This, Recanati says, is what typically happens in discourse. For example, we can start with an assertion about a certain place, such as "Berkeley is a nice place", and then we can go on with the description of the city by saying, for example, "there are bookstores and coffee shops everywhere": in this case Berkeley disappears from the explicit content of my thought and I only focus on a smaller situation and aspect of Berkeley. Once again, Recanati remarks, this change in the content implies a change in the situation of evaluation, which in the former case could be identified, perhaps, with the United States, or with some other university city, whereas in the latter case consists of Berkeley itself (2000: 67-68). To sum up:

> In reflection we step out of the current exercised situation and adopt a reflective stance towards it, construing it as an entity comprised in the new exercised situation. In projection we focus on an entity comprised in the exercised situation up to the point where it becomes the exercised situation and is no longer represented as an entity: only the entities which *it* comprises are represented. (2000: 78)

As adults, Recanati argues, we are capable of dealing with both kinds of representation: those by means of which we represent a certain state of affairs (that is, the entities that constitute a certain situation) and those by means of which we represent a certain situation as an entity, and thus, as part of a wider state of affairs; moreover, we become able to rapidly shift from one kind of representation to the other.

Now, the distinction between these two kinds of thoughts also concerns our imaginary representations, so that we can distinguish between what we could call *simulative* states and *metarepresentational* states. More precisely, if a simulative state can be described as a thought *concerning* an imaginary situation[1], a metarepresentational state is defined as a thought which *is about* an imaginary situation, but which *concerns* a real situation (2000: 81). By appealing to the Austinian semantics originally proposed by Barwise and Etchemendy (1987), Recanati thus distinguishes the two following logical forms (cf. 2000: 81):

(1) $[s] \models_w \sigma$
(2) $[s'] \models_@ « s \models_w \sigma »$

---

1   For the specific definition of an 'imaginary situation' given by Recanati, cf. 2000: § 5.4.

The former corresponds to a simulative state, where the fact σ, which is the content of the state, is supported ($\models$) by the situation s, which belongs to an imaginary world (w). The latter corresponds, instead, to a metarepresentational thought. In this case what the metarepresentation depicts is the fact that a certain imaginary situation s supports a certain fact σ, but this content, represented in double angle brackets («s $\models_w$ σ») is supported, in turn, by a situation s', which belongs to the actual world (@). In this sense, the two cognitive processes of reflection and projection can be described, respectively, as the passage from entertaining a first-order representation with form (1) to entertaining a second-order representation with form (2) and, vice versa, the passage from (2) to (1).

Now, according to Recanati, the distinction between these two logical structures would correspond also to the distinction between two different steps in a child's cognitive development. Children, in other words, would first learn to deal with first-order representations of imaginary situations – what typically happens in pretense play – and would come to understand metarepresentational structures only later, between the third and the fourth year of life, as soon as they become able to pass the false-belief task. Before that age, in fact, children do not dispose of the notion of representation, so they are unable to represent a certain fact – be it real or imaginary – as *supported* by a certain situation. This means, according to Recanati's account, that the child would first be able "to entertain imaginary situations 'from within'," thus representing first-order facts of the kind: [s] $\models_w$ σ, and only later would acquire "the ability to state objective facts *about* imaginary situations", thus becoming able to manipulate more complicated structures of the kind: [s'] $\models_@$ «s $\models_w$ σ» (2000: 81).

As Recanati recognizes, however, pretense play poses a problem for this two-stages account since, in pretense play, children learn to deal with imaginary and genuine representations at the same time, far before having acquired the capacity to form metarepresentational states. The same concept is expressed by Perner by appealing to the notion of "mental model". Around the age of 18 months, Perner says, the child becomes a "situation theorist": she abandons a single model of reality and starts to build models also for non-actual states of affairs such as goals, imaginary situations, past situations, etc. (1991: 47). Moreover, the child is not only able to build up different models, but she is also able to compare the present situation with a past one, or an imaginary scenario with the actual one (1991: 66). This cognitive change is what causes the emergence of several new skills, among them the ability to engage in and understand pretense but, Perner recognizes, it also requires from the child the possession of an integrating

model, that is, a model by means of which the child can compare representations concerning different situations (e.g. her model of reality with that
of pretense, cf. 1991: 9, 54, 66).

As seen, however, whereas in Perner the recognition of the need for an integrating model does not imply the attribution of some metarepresentational
ability (cf. IV.3), Recanati interprets this capacity for comparing different
representations as implying the mastering of a complex, metarepresenta-
tional structure of the form: [s'] $\models_@$ « s $\models_w$ σ » (2000: 82). For example, in a
pretend scenario such as the banana-like-a-telephone, what the child would
entertain, according to Recanati, is the following integrating model:

> *Pretend-reality model*
> [s'] $\models_@$ « real situation $\models_@$ « that object is a banana » »
> [s'] $\models_@$ « pretend situation $\models_w$ « that object is a telephone » »

The child would thus be able to represent, at the same time, two different facts (both supported by the situation s', which is the actual situation
the child is in): the fact that *in reality* the object in front of her is a banana,
and the fact that *in pretense* the object in front of her is a telephone (2000:
86). The child would thus not only be able to represent a certain fact (e.g.
"that object is a banana", or "that object is a telephone") as *supported* by a
certain (imaginary or real) situation but, Recanati stresses, imaginary scenarios would be treated by children as patterns of the real situation they
are in, in the sense that they would be represented by children as facts contained in the same situation which also contains real-world facts (the situation s'). Still, Recanati suggests, children would perceive these imaginary
situations as endowed with some special property:

> [...] imaginary situations are treated on the pattern of real situations: they
> are part of the world, but they have special properties which distinguish them
> from the other situations. Imaginary situations are like ghosts who are part of
> the actual world but exhibit funny properties (e.g. invisibility and penetrabil-
> ity). (2000: 83)

In particular, Recanati says, children would be especially sensitive to
one property of imaginary situations, that is: their *hyperinsulation* (2000:
ibidem). Hyperinsulation is tied to the phenomenon of persistence or non-
persistence of certain quantificational facts. Persistent facts are those facts
that, if they hold in a certain situation s, they surely will also hold in the
enlarged situation s', containing s. To take Recanati's example, if it is a fact
that there is a man in this room who is happy, it will also be a fact that there

is a man in this building who is happy. On the contrary, if it is a fact that all men in this room are happy, it is not necessarily a fact that all men in this building are happy. This is a non-persistent fact, and this is why every situation must be considered as

> a micro-universe, closed upon itself and insulated from other micro-universes. It is insulated because, and to the extent that, the facts which hold within a particular situation do not necessarily hold outside that situation [...]. (2000: 78)

Now, Recanati claims, imaginary situations are not only insulated in the sense just specified, but they are hyperinsulated, in the sense that all kinds of quantificational facts holding in an imaginary situation are non-persistent. If I imagine that there is a dwarf in this room, it does not follow that there is a dwarf in the real situation which contains the imaginary one (that is, in the real world in which I am pretending). Imaginary facts, in other words, are supported by imaginary situations, not by the real situations which contain the imaginary ones. According to Recanati, even very young children would be sensitive to this property of imaginary situations, whose recognition would help them to keep these representations distinct from actual ones.

Meini and Voltolini (2010), however, have criticized this solution, claiming that the integrating model proposed by Recanati is too demanding for children younger than the age of 3 or 4. As seen, according to the kind of integrating model proposed by Recanati (the *Pretend-reality model*), the child would be able to depict at the same time two different and complex facts, and she would understand that these facts are supported by two different situations, a real and a pretend one:

$$[s'] \models_@ \text{« real situation } \models_@ \text{« that object is a banana » »}$$
$$[s'] \models_@ \text{« pretend situation } \models_w \text{« that object is a telephone » »}$$

But, Meini and Voltolini claim, if things were so, then the theory of pretense proposed by Recanati would require a strong metarepresentational ability. In the integrating model, in fact, the pretend model (« pretend situation $\models_w$ « that object is a telephone » ») is *nested* in the reality model (s'), but such nesting is precisely what occurs when "from outside a fiction, we speak of that very fiction"[2]. When we say that "In fiction F, *p*", what we are expressing is precisely a representation of the form:

---

2   This is, Meini and Voltolini specify, the typical case but, of course, we could speak about a fiction from the perspective of another fiction: as when we say, for

[s'] $\models_@$ « pretend situation $\models_w$ « p » »

For example:

[s'] $\models_@$ « Conan Doyle's stories $\models_w$ « Holmes smokes a pipe » »

In other words, we are depicting a certain fact ("Holmes smokes a pipe") as supported by a certain imaginary situation – in this case, the stories ideated by Arthur Conan Doyle. This idea of pretense thus requires that the pretender be capable of representing at least the supporting relation ($\models_w$) which exists between a certain mental content and a certain situation, and representing a mental content as supported by a certain situation implies, if not the explicit employment of the concept of representation, at least that the pretender understands what a representation is, and, in particular, the fact that a representation can depict something which is different from reality. This kind of Pernerian account, Meini and Voltolini thus conclude (cf. 2010: §5), is heavily metarepresentationalist, since it implies that children are able, as early as the second year of their life, to understand what a representation is and how it works, even if they still do not possess the concept of a representation.

1.2. *Some space for a weaker account*

As we have seen in § IV.4, Meini and Voltolini (2010) have proposed an account of the metarepresentational abilities that are involved in pretense which relies on an important distinction between two ways of representing a representation. More precisely, Meini and Voltolini argue, one can represent a representation:

(1) *qua* representation, thus mobilizing the notion of representation in the very content of the metarepresentational thought;

(2) or *qua* a mere instantiation of the relation of representing.

This distinction is understood as a distinction between general and singular thoughts, that is, a distinction between thoughts which are about a notion and thoughts which are about an individual. In the case of second-order thoughts, we can then speak of:

---

example, that "Atreius loses his horse Atrax in the Swamps of Sadness", thus speaking about the world of *Fantasia*, whose story is contained in the book read by the protagonist of the *NeverEnding Story*. This, however, has no influence on the point that we are making here.

(1) *general* metarepresentations, which are about the *notion* of representation itself;

(2) *singular* metarepresentations, which are about *a given representation* without, at the same time, recognizing that representation as a representation.

These two ways of representing a representation, the authors also argue, correspond to two main stages in the child's development. More precisely, children would first acquire the ability to represent a representation in this minimal sense of entertaining a singular thought of the kind: "*this* is F", where "this" refers to a certain representational content. Only later, between the third and fourth year of life, would children acquire the notion of representation, thus becoming able to entertain general thoughts of the kind: "S pretends that this *representation* is F".

Now, as anticipated, what I want to argue is that a SMR theory of pretense is not committed to embracing a strong metarepresentational account like the one proposed by Recanati, but it is also compatible with a two-stage account like the one proposed by Meini and Voltolini. In order to see this, let us recall, first of all, the cognitive situation that characterizes, according to the SMR account, a pretending subject.

As we have seen, the SMR architecture of the mind envisages two main categories of mental states: those which are entertained in the egocentric mode, and those which are entertained in the anaphoric mode, the critical difference between them consisting of the fact that, whereas the states in the egocentric mode do not require that we explicitly represent the situations concerned by them, this representation is necessarily required by our anaphoric states. In other words, when a subject entertains a state in the anaphoric mode, she represents not only a certain content, but she must also entertain some other representation, which depicts the situation against which that state has to be evaluated. Now, the question is: how much awareness of her own cognitive situation must the subject possess? In particular, in the case of pretense, must the pretender recognize her mental states as *representations* of certain kinds? And must she necessarily represent the situation concerned by her anaphoric state as the *situation of evaluation* for that given state? And thus, must she be aware of the *supporting relation* itself, that is, that a certain fact is made true by a certain situation? I maintain that the SMR framework does not compel us to attribute any of these skills to the pretender.

What the relativist account claims is simply that if one entertains a representation in the anaphoric mode, his or her representation must be accompanied by some other mental state, which is cognitively salient to his or her mind, and whose content consists in the situation against which that representation has to be evaluated. This, however, does not mean that the pretender must recognize which kind of relation subsists between her states, nor must she recognize her anaphoric representation as a representation and, moreover, as a representation *supported* or *made true* by a certain state of affairs. I think, rather, that the minimal capacity the pretender is supposed to possess is that of being able to *relativize* her anaphoric representations to some other representations. In other words:

> [...] regardless of the way the young child effectively conceptualises what (s)he is entertaining, (s)he acknowledges *of* the two 'things' that (s)he is entertaining that they are differently located. As has already been stated, this is enough for his/her mind to be metarepresentational, even if only at the *singular* level: the child acknowledges that *this* – which is a representation of the 'real' model – is not be ranked with *that* – which is a representation of the 'imaginary' model. (Meini & Voltolini 2010: 49)

As in the account of pretense given by Meini and Voltolini, also in an SMR account, I claim, the subject who pretends must simply possess the minimal capacity to 'rank,' as Meini and Voltolini say, her pretend representations with those other representations which depict the situation concerned by them, as well as to keep them separate from those which depict, instead, different scenarios. All a pretender must be able to do, in other words, is to represent certain mental contents (the contents of the anaphoric states) as contents which go together with certain other contents (a certain world, a certain time, a certain space) and this capacity implies only singular metarepresentations: it is a capacity to represent a certain mental content as 'close' or 'relative' to certain other contents and as distinct from other kinds of content (such as our perceptual contents). To put it differently, the pretending subject does not have to be able to entertain a complex representation of the kind: [s'] $\models_@$ « pretend situation $\models_w$ « that object is a telephone » », but only to understand that the representation [s] $\models_w$ « that object is a telephone » is differently located with respect to the representation [s'] $\models_@$ « that object is a banana » and has to be ranked, instead, with other representations such as [s] $\models_w$ « mama is calling grandma ».

In this sense, an SMR account is able to specify exactly what that 'minimally metarepresentational capacity' consists in: it is a capacity to relativize to or rank one's own pretend representations with those representations which depict the situation they concern, thus keeping them distinct from genuine mental states or other pretend representations which concern a different situation.

2. *A Strong Moderate Relativist account of pretense*

2.1. *Redescribing pretense*

As we have seen in the previous chapter (cf. § 3.2), Recanati distinguishes, after Perry, two different cognitive situations: one in which there is an "external guarantee" that our present representation concerns the *hic et nunc* situation – the situation in which this representation is tokened – and one in which this external guarantee is missing. For example, a state of perception necessarily concerns the *hic et nunc* situation because of its causal genesis, that is, because of the way it arises and its content is determined. This guarantee is lacking, however, in the case of imagination, or memory. In these cases, Recanati claims, the situation concerned by our representation is not determined by some external fact, but rather, by some other mental state of ours.

This, of course, applies also to the imaginings we employ in pretense. More precisely, as seen, in pretense it seems that we are dealing at the same time with different representations: on one hand, we certainly have some egocentric representations that concern the *hic et nunc* situation (i.e. our perceptual judgments); on the other hand, we are also imagining another situation, that is, we also have some representations entertained in the anaphoric mode. In order to clarify, we can start by describing in the SMR framework some of the examples of pretense that we have considered before (cf. § I.1).

Let us take, for instance, the first experimental setting described by Leslie (1987), the banana-like-a-telephone scenario. According to the account I am proposing, the child playing this game of make-believe would possess, at the same time, two different representations: a perceptual judgment with content "that is a banana", and a pretend representation with content "that is a telephone". But whereas the former would be entertained in the egocentric mode (since the situation concerned by the state is determined by the external environment), the latter would be entertained in the anaphoric mode. This means that, in representing the propositional content "that is a telephone", the child not only entertains this state, but she also represents, in some other mental state, the situation concerned by this content (for example, the child could be representing a possible world in which mama is making a telephone call to grandma).

The same treatment can be applied to the tea-party scenario (Leslie 1994). In this case, again, what the child is dealing with are two representations: one in the egocentric and the other in the anaphoric mode. The only difference with respect to the first example is the fact that the content of the two representations is perfectly identical: in both examples, the child is thinking that there is a cup which possesses the property of being empty. But, again, whereas in one case the situation concerned by this personal proposition is determined by what the child is actually seeing and it is not explicitly represented by the bearer of the state, in the other case it is determined by some other state of hers (a state which depicts the fact that she is having a tea party, in the course of which some tea has been poured into a cup, and then the cup has been turned upside down). So, we end up with two states with the same content p ("That cup is empty"), but in one case the state is entertained in the egocentric mode, in the other case it is anaphorically linked to another representation.

Finally, the relativist account can be applied to the third kind of pretense that we have outlined, i.e. the case in which I do not represent something in place of something else, but I represent the existence of a new object, thus pretending to add, so to say, a new element to the ontological furnishing of the actual world (cf. § I.1.4). For example, in the case in which I pretend that my teddy bear has a hat on his head, I can describe myself as holding two different representations: a real perception of my teddy bear (with no hat on his head) and a pretend representation of my teddy bear with a hat on his head. The former representation is held in the egocentric mode; the latter is instead in the anaphoric mode, and thus possesses a link to some other representation of mine (for example, the representation of a possible world in which I received this bear as a gift from my uncle).

By relying on the description of the games of make-believe given so far, we can now reconsider in more detail some features of pretense and the way in which they can be explained within a relativist framework.

2.2. *Some features revised*

Given the basic assumption that pretense always requires one to entertain two different states – an anaphoric and an egocentric state – we can now explore in greater detail how the main features of pretense can be redescribed in a relativist account such as the one I am proposing. We can start with what Nichols and Stich have defined as the *initial premise*.

2.2.1. *The initial premise*

As seen (cf. § I.1.3), according to Nichols and Stich the initial premise basically consists of one or more assumptions – shared by all participants in the game of make-believe – which contribute to defining the context of pretense. For example, in the empty-cup scenario, the child is explicitly required to pour some tea into a cup and to offer it to the experimenter. Since there is no real tea to pour, however, the child plausibly understands that the experimenter is not speaking seriously and that it is an act of play she is asked to engage in. As a consequence, Nichols and Stich say, a representation with content "we are going to have a tea party" is stored in the child's Possible Worlds Box. From this representation, and by relying on her previous knowledge about tea parties, the child can draw some inferences about what is going to happen in the course of the pretense (e.g. "we will eat some cakes"), thus adding some new representations to the PWB.

According to my account, however, the role played by the initial premise is even more important. The representations contained in the PWB, in fact, not only share the feature of being all in the anaphoric mode, but each representation contributes to determining the concerning relation of the other representations that are stored in the Box. For example, a representation like "we are going to have a tea party", once put in the PWB at the beginning of the pretense episode, would constitute the cognitive background of the subsequent pretend representations. So, when the child takes a cup and pretends to pour some tea into it, the content of her pretend state ("I am filling the cup with some tea") must be evaluated with respect to the situation depicted by the former representation (an imaginary situation in which she is going to have a tea party). When, after having pretended to fill the cup, she pretends to drink from it, again, the content "I am drinking some tea" necessarily concerns a situation in which she is having a tea party and has poured some tea into her cup, and so on. In this sense, then, every representation stored in the PWB contributes to determining the situation that will be concerned by the following representations that will be produced in the course of the pretense episode.

One could object, however, that on this account we can never speak of an initial premise because the fact of entertaining an anaphoric state always implies that one entertains – in addition to a certain mental content – another state, which represents the situation concerned by the former. In other words, since the initial premise is the representation of an imaginary state of affairs, and thus must be in the anaphoric mode, the initial premise must also be anaphorically linked to another representation; this, of course, gives rise to an infinite regress.

This, however, is not necessarily the case. As seen in the previous section (§ 2.1), when the child is asked to pour some tea in a cup but there is no tea at all to pour, the child presumably infers that she is engaging in a game. So she must be aware, at least, of the fact that the representation "I am pouring tea in the cup" does not concern reality, it is not valid in the actual world, but only in the game in which she is engaging. To follow Meini and Voltolini's suggestion, every pretender must be aware, at least, of the fact that her pretend representations are "distinctly located" with respect to her genuine ones. Now, in a relativist framework this kind of knowledge can be interpreted as the capacity to understand that "this (e.g. the pretend mental content 'I am pouring tea in the cup') is F", where F can stand for the property of existing in the game, in a world different from the actual one. In other words, according to our account, if a pretender recognizes something as pretense, she not only entertains a non-actual content, but she possesses the minimal capacity to understand that this content is relative to a certain world, *distinct* from the actual one.

2.2.2. *Cognitive quarantine*

The relativist account we are endorsing can help us to explain another important feature of pretense: namely, the *cognitive quarantine* of our pretend representations.

As we have seen in detail in chapter 2, this question constitutes an important matter of debate among the different cognitive theories of pretense. On one hand, Nichols and Stich explain this phenomenon by appealing to the fact that pretend representations are a special kind of mental state, characterized by their peculiar functional role; but, in doing so, they encounter severe problems explaining why pretend representations have the same effects as their genuine counterparts (beliefs) on some of our cognitive mechanisms. The Single Code Hypothesis, introduced to solve just this problem, is not convincing because it is not at all clear what this Code could consist of. On the other hand, the position we have labeled as "recreativism" supposes that, for every kind of mental state, we can reproduce a copy of that state, i.e. a representation which possesses the same internal functional role characteristic of that type of mental state. Recreativism, however, is called upon to explain how pretend representations can be kept distinct from our genuine ones, i.e. how we can deal, at the same time, with representations that share not only the same content, but also the same internal functional role, without getting confused.

The adoption of the SMR framework, I have already pointed out, can help us to solve this problem, that is, it can help us explain why two identical mental states, endowed with the same content, can have different consequences on our behavior and, at the same time, can be kept distinct by the subject. As we have seen, entertaining a non-actual content in a SMR framework means to entertain an anaphoric state: to entertain, that is, a certain content while being aware of the fact that this content concerns a situation different from the actual one. In this way, our pretend representations are quarantined because they are always accompanied by the minimal consciousness of being 'differently located,' subsisting in a situation different from the actual one.

Moreover, I want to claim, a SMR theory of the mind allows us to revise the account of pretense proposed by Nichols and Stich (2000) without incurring the problems that typically afflicted their theory. What I want to argue is that, by relying on a relativist account, one is able to explain why some mechanisms treat our pretend and genuine representations in the same manner, whereas other mechanisms do not, without postulating the existence of a mysterious entity like the Single Code.

According to my hypothesis, not all cognitive mechanisms are sensitive to the same properties of the representations they deal with. More precisely, whereas some mechanisms may be sensitive only to the contents of our representations (what our representations *are about*), other mechanisms may be sensitive to other properties as well, such as the anaphoric link subsisting between certain mental contents. Our inference mechanisms are a typical example of the former: they treat different occurrences of the same representation (e.g. "that cup is empty" or "that is a telephone") in exactly the same manner[3], independently of whether the representation in question is a genuine or a pretend one. On the contrary, our Action-control systems seem to also be sensitive to the fact that the representations they receive as input possess an anaphoric link to some other mental representations: when the representation in question is entertained in the egocentric mode, the systems go on with their computations and give rise to an action; when, instead, the representation is entertained in the anaphoric mode – and thus it implies some minimal form of metarepresentation – the action is typically inhibited, or at least it is not computed in an automatic way.

In this sense, what I am proposing is to reverse Nichols and Stich's perspective. Nichols and Stich have introduced the Single Code, a property shared by pretend and genuine representations, in order to assure that they be treated in the same manner by some of our cognitive mechanisms. On

---

3   As already said, according to our account, the only level of content which can play the role of the psychological content is the meaning of the sentence-type. So, from a psychological point of view, two occurrences of the thought "that cup is empty" express exactly the same thought.

the contrary, I suppose that pretend and genuine representations endowed with the same content are treated, by default, in the same manner by our cognitive mechanisms. Some mechanisms, however, do not, because they are sensitive to metarepresentations, they are sensitive, that is, to the fact that pretend representations are always tied to some other representations (those depicting the situation concerned by the former).

One could ask, however, whether this relativist account can also be compatible with a recreativist position. A recreativist could claim that we can entertain not only our beliefs in the anaphoric mode, but also our desires, our perceptions, and, more generally, that all states that can be entertained in the egocentric mode can be entertained also in the anaphoric mode. In other words, belief-like imaginings, desire-like imaginings, perception-like imaginings, etc., could be all understood as states belonging to the super-category of anaphoric states.

As I have shown in chapter 3, however, I have independent reasons to deny the existence of – at least – desire-like- and emotion-like states, and these reasons become even clearer if we interpret the recreativist position from a relativist point of view. Let us first consider the case of desires.

At the end of chapter 3, I argued that, if one adopts a theory of desire like the one proposed by Carruthers (2006), then one is compelled to deny the existence of pretend desires. According to Carruthers' account, in fact, desires are to be understood as representational states and, more precisely, as representations of non-actual states of affairs which are processed by our motivational systems and which are 'marked' by them with a positive feeling, thus possessing certain motivational power. Now, such a definition excludes *a priori* the existence of pretend desires, since both genuine and pretend desires (that is, both the desires that we have in real-world contexts and those that we have in pretense) are representations of non-actual states of affairs endowed with a certain motivating power. If we 'translate' this theory into the SMR framework, this is tantamount to saying that, when we entertain a desire, we necessarily entertain a representational state in the anaphoric mode, which has certain effects on our motivational systems. So, in this sense, we cannot speak of pretend desires as the 'anaphoric counterpart' of some states in the egocentric mode, since genuine desires are also anaphoric states, that is, representations of a situation different from the *hic et nunc*.

The situation is slightly different in the case of emotions, since our emotional reactions can be activated both by a representation of the *hic et nunc* situation and by one of a non-actual state of affairs. In this sense we could distinguish between genuine emotions – emotions that are caused by some egocentric state – and pretend emotions – those that are activated by some anaphoric state. As we have remarked (cf. § III.2.4), however, it is not clear at all that in the case of our emotions the epistemic-cognitive state that constitutes their causal antecedent must necessarily be a defining criterion of the emotions themselves. As we have seen, at least for the most basic emotions, it seems that the presence of an epistemic-cognitive state cannot be considered an identifying criterion for the emotions themselves, otherwise we would end up with a wide range of affective reactions – such as the emotions felt by animals and infants, but also those cases of inappropriate and vicarious emotions – that we could not truly define as 'emotions.' Independently of the fact that an emotion is caused either by an egocentric or by an anaphoric representation, then, it seems that these states are not involved in the definition of the emotion itself, and thus, again, the distinction between genuine and pretend emotions does not make any sense.

This is why our account cannot be assimilated into a recreativist account and why I favor, instead, Nichols and Stich's account of pretense, claiming that a relativist account of our mental states can help solve this theory's main problem: that of explaining the different cognitive significance of pretend and genuine representations, and the fact that these representations are not confused.

2.2.3. Anchoring

As we have seen in § I.1.3, another crucial feature of pretense is the anchorage of pretend representations to reality, or better, to specific aspects of the here-and-now situation. For example, when the child pretends that a banana is a telephone, her pretend representation "that is a telephone" is clearly anchored to the banana that is in her hands, that is, to the genuine perception "that is a banana". But what does it mean, exactly, that the pretend representation is anchored to another representation, in particular with respect to the architecture of the mind involved? In a SMR framework like the one I have sketched, answering this question amounts to answering the question: how is the pretend (and thus anaphoric) representation "that is a telephone" related to the perceptual (and thus egocentric) representation "that is a banana"? In other words, which is the relation between the two mental contents?

In order to answer this question, it is important, first of all, to recognize that both thoughts concerned are demonstrative thoughts, thoughts which contain a demonstrative element. For example, as already seen in the previous chapter (cf. V.2.1), the content of a perception like seeing a flower can be described as the proposition "there is a flower *there*", where the demonstrative "there" means a certain place to which the bearer of the thought is demonstratively related. Analogously, if I pretend that "there is a puppy *there*", the content of my thought is the proposition that "there is a puppy *there*", where "there" means, again, a certain place to which the bearer of the thought is demonstratively related. The difference is that, whereas in the former case there is an external guarantee that the reference of "there" concerns our locale, in the latter case its reference is determined by the thought to which the pretend perception is anaphorically linked. In other words, the place to which "there" refers is represented in the bearer's mind or, as said, it is "cognitively salient" to her mind.

To put it differently, when two thoughts – an egocentric and an anaphoric one – are anchored one to the other, then their contents – which correspond to the respective meanings of the sentence-type – are 'overlapping', in the sense that they share the same demonstrative element. The pretending subject, however, is aware that this same demonstrative element refers in one case to a certain place or object in the real world, in the other case to another place or object she is presently thinking about.

3. *Pretense and mindreading*

Before concluding, I would like to make some final remarks about the three notions from which this investigation has moved: imagination, pretense and mindreading. In chapter 5 we clarified how imagination should be understood in the SMR framework and which kind of mental architecture it requires. Now, since imagination is involved both in pretense and mindreading, we could thus conclude that one and the same kind of mental state is involved in these two activities. The question, however, is: is there something which is peculiar to mindreading or to pretense? Of course, one difference certainly consists in the fact that, as seen previously, the imaginings involved in pretense – what we properly call "pretend mental states" – are anchored to some aspect in the here-and-now. But, is there something else which concerns the content itself of these states?

As seen in § V.3.4, imaginings can be described as the kinds of state that can be anaphoric for every aspect of the situation of evaluation, that is, a state that can differ from the *hic et nunc* situation in every aspect whatsoever. So, we could start by asking: is this true for both the kind of imaginings involved in pretense and for those involved in mindreading?

The answer is affirmative, but with a restriction in the case of pretense: more precisely, these imaginings are always anaphoric for the aspect of the world, but the world concerned by these states is necessarily a possible world, different from the actual one. When I imagine about a fictional context, in other words, what I am always aware of is that my pretend contents concern a possible world, different from the actual one. On the contrary, this is not necessarily true in the case of mindreading. Of course, I could try to imagine what Anna Karenina was feeling in the moments just before her decision to jump under the train. In this case, for example, I could rehearse an emotion of sorrow, or desperation, knowing, at the same time, that these feelings concern not myself but this fictional character, and thus knowing that they concern a fictional world. This is clearly different from a typical exercise in mindreading, as when I try to understand what a friend of mine is thinking at the moment, but it is also different from the case we examined in the previous chapter (cf. § V.3.4), the case, that is, in which I try to imagine how Napoleon was feeling before the battle of Waterloo. Also in this case, even if I am ascribing certain (first-person) thoughts to a person different from myself and living in a different time, the world concerned by these states is, however, the actual world.

The kinds of pretend mental states involved in mindreading are thus more 'free' than those involved in pretense, in the sense that they can also concern our world (the actual world), and not only some possible world.

Summary of the chapter

In this final chapter I have offered a relativist theory of pretense, trying to outline the reasons why I favor such an account. By adopting a relativist framework like the one proposed by Recanati, I have been able to develop a cognitive architecture of the mind which allows us to solve some of the typical problems that afflict other theories of pretense, such as the explanation of the cognitive quarantine of our pretend representations. In particular, as I have tried to show, it is possible to reinterpret the theory of pretense proposed by Nichols and Stich (2000) within a relativist framework, substituting the obscure Single-Code theory with the more warranted notion of an anaphoric link between representations.

Moreover, I have claimed that our relativist theory of pretense does not require the strong form of metarepresentation to which Recanati makes appeal in his *Oratio Obliqua, Oratio Recta*, but is compatible with a minimally metarepresentational account like the one proposed by Meini and

Voltolini. In my view, what the pretending child is required to do in order to pretend, is neither to be able to master the notion of representation, nor to explicitly represent that a certain fact is supported by a certain imaginary situation. Rather, a pretender must possess at least the minimal capacity to relativize certain mental contents to a background knowledge, thus keeping them separate from other states.

REFERENCES

Anderson J.D. (1996), *The Reality of Illusion: An Ecological Approach to Cognitive Film Theory*, Carbondale and Edwardsville, Southern Illinois University Press

Baron-Cohen, S. (1994), "The Mindreading System: new directions for research", *Current Psychology of Cognition*, 13: 724-750

Baron-Cohen S. (1995), *Mindblindness: an essay on autism and theory of mind*, Cambridge (MA), The MIT Press

Baron-Cohen S., Leslie A.M., Frith U. (1995), "Does the autistic child have a theory of mind?", *Cognitive Psychology*, 21: 37-46

Barwise J., Etchemendy J. (1987), *The Liar: An Essay on Truth and Circularity*, New York, Oxford University Press

Barwise J., Perry J. (1983), *Situations and Attitudes*, Cambridge (MA), The MIT Press / Bradford Books

Bechara A., Damasio A.R., Damasio H., Anderson S.W. (1994), "Insensitivity to future consequences following damage to human prefrontal cortex", *Cognition*, 50: 7-15

Bisiach E., Luzzatti C. (1978), "Unilateral Neglect of Representational Space", *Cortex*, 14: 129-133

Carruthers P. (2006), "Why Pretend?", in S. Nichols (ed.), *The Architecture of the Imagination*, Oxford, Clarendon Press: 89-109

Currie G. (1990), *The nature of fiction*, Cambridge, Cambridge University Press

Currie G. (1995), "Visual imagery as the simulation of vision", *Mind & Language*, 10: 25-44

Currie G. (1997), "The Paradox of Caring", in M. Hjort and S. Laver (eds.), *Emotion and the Arts*, New York, Oxford University Press: 63-77

Currie G. (1998), "Pretence, pretending and metarepresenting", *Mind & Language*, 13(1): 35-55

Currie G. (2002), "Imagination and make-believe", in B. Gaut and D. McIver Lopes (eds.), *The Routledge Companion to Aesthetics*, London, Routledge

Currie G., Ravenscroft I. (1997), "Mental simulation and motor imagery", *Philosophy of Science*, 64: 161-180

Currie G., Ravenscroft I. (2002), *Recreative Minds*, Oxford, Clarendon Press

Damasio A.R. (1994), *Descartes' Error: Emotion, Reason, and the Human Brain*, New York, Grosset/Putnam

Dennett D.C. (1969), *Content and Consciousness*, London, Routledge and Kegan Paul
Dennett D.C. (1987), *The Intentional Stance*, Cambridge (MA), The MIT Press
Dominey P., Decety J., Brouselle E., Chazot G., Jeannerod M. (1995), "Motor Imagery of a Lateralized Sequential Task is Asymmetrically Slowed in Hemi-Parkinson's Patients", *Neuropsychologia*, 33: 727-741
Evans G. (1982), *The Varieties of Reference*, ed. by J. McDowell, Oxford, Clarendon Press
Fodor J. (1975), *The Language of Thought*, New York, Crowell
Fodor J. (1983), *The Modularity of Mind*, Cambridge (MA), The MIT Press
Friedman O., Leslie A.M. (2007), "The conceptual underpinnings of pretense: Pretending is not behaving-as-if", *Cognition*, 105(1): 103-124
Funkhouser E., Spaulding S. (2009), "Imagination and other scripts", *Philosophical Studies*, 143: 291-314
Goldman A.I. (1989), "Interpretation Psychologized", *Mind & Language*; then in M. Davies and T. Stone (eds.), *Folk Psychology: the Theory of Mind Debate*, Oxford, Blackwell, 1995a: 74-99
Goldman A.I. (1993), "The psychology of folk psychology", *Behavioral and Brain Sciences*, 16: 15-28
Goldman A.I. (2006a), "Imagination and Simulation in Audience Responses to Fiction", in S. Nichols (ed.), *The Architecture of the Imagination*, Oxford, Clarendon Press: 41-56
Goldman A.I. (2006b), *Simulating Minds*, Oxford, Oxford University Press
Gopnik A., Meltzoff A.N. (1997), *Words, Thoughts, and Theories*, Cambridge (MA), The MIT Press
Gordon R. (1986), "Folk psychology as simulation", *Mind & Language*, 1: 158-171; then in M. Davies and T. Stone (eds.), *Folk Psychology: the Theory of Mind Debate*, Oxford, Blackwell, 1995a: 60-73
Gordon R. (1995), "Simulation without introspection or inference from me to you", in M. Davies and T. Stone (eds.), *Mental Simulation*, Oxford, Blackwell, 1995b: 53-67
Gordon R., Barker J. (1994), "Autism and the 'theory of mind' debate", in G. Graham and G.L. Stephens (eds.), *Philosophical psychopathology: a book of readings*, Cambridge (MA), The MIT Press
Greenspan P. (1988), *Emotions and Reasons: An Inquiry Into Emotional Justification*, New York, Routledge, Chapman and Hall
Hannay A. (1971), *Mental Images: A Defence*, New York, Humanities Press Inc.
Harris P.L. (1989), *Children and emotions. The development of psychological understanding*, Oxford, Blackwell
Harris P.L. (1994), "Understanding pretense", in C. Lewis and P. Mitchell (eds.), *Children's understanding of mind: Origins and development*, Hove (UK), Lawrence Erlbaum Associates: 235-259
Harris P.L. (1995a), "From Simulation to Folk Psychology: The Case for Development", in M. Davis and T. Stone (eds.), *Folk Psychology: the Theory of Mind Debate*, Oxford, Blackwell, 1995a: 207-231

Harris P.L. (1995b), "Imagining and pretending", in M. Davies and T. Stone (eds.), *Mental Simulation*, Oxford, Blackwell, 1995b: 170-184

Harris P.L., Kavanaugh, R.D. (1993), *Young children's understanding of pretense*, *Monographs of the Society for Research in Child Development*, 58(1)

Heal J. (1986), "Replication and functionalism", in J. Butterfield (ed.), *Language, Mind, and Logic*, Cambridge, Cambridge University Press

Huttenlocher J., Higgins E.T. (1978), "Issues in the Study of Symbolic Development", in W. Collins (ed.), *Minnesota Symposia on Child Psychology*, Hillsdale (NJ), Lawrence Erlbaum Associates, vol. 11: 98-140

Kahneman D., Tversky A. (1982), "The simulation heuristic", in D. Kahneman, P. Slovic and A. Tversky (eds.), *Judgement under uncertainty: Heuristics and biases*, New York, Cambridge University Press: 201-208

Kaplan D. (1989), "Demonstratives", in J. Almog, J. Perry and H. Wettstein (eds.), *Themes from Kaplan*, New York, Oxford University Press: 481-563

Korta K. (2007), review of F. Recanati, *Perspectival Though. A Plea for (Moderate) Relativism*, *Notre Dame Philosophical Reviews*, published on-line 04.07.08, http://ndpr.nd.edu/review.cfm?id=13486

Leslie A.M. (1987), "Pretense and representation: The origins of 'theory of mind'", *Psychological Review*, 94: 412-426

Leslie A.M. (1994), "Pretending and believing: issues in the theory of ToMM", *Cognition*, 50: 211-238

Levinson J. (1990), "The Place of Real Emotion in Response to Fictions", *The Journal of Aesthetics and Art Criticism*, 48: 79-80

Lewis D. (1978), "Truth in Fiction", *American Philosophical Quarterly*, 15: 37-46; reprinted in Id., *Philosophical Papers, Volume 1*, New York, Oxford University Press, 1983: 261-280

Lillard A.S. (1993a), "Pretend play skills and the child's theory of mind", *Child Development*, 64: 348-371

Lillard A.S. (1993b), "Young children's conceptualization of pretense: Action or mental representational state?", *Child Development*, 64: 372-386

Lillard A.S. (1994), "Making sense of pretence", in C. Lewis and P. Mitchell (eds.), *Children's early understanding of mind: Origins and development*, Hove (UK), Lawrence Erlbaum Associates: 211-234

Lillard A.S. (2001), "Pretend play as Twin Earth: A social-cognitive analysis", *Developmental Review*, 21: 495-531

Lyons W. (1984), "The tiger and his stripes", *Analysis*, 44(2): 93-95

McDowell J. (1982), "Truth-Value Gaps", in L.J. Cohen, J. Łó H. Pfeiffer and K.P. Podewski (eds.), *Logic, Methodology and Philosophy of Science VI: Proceedings of the Sixth International Congress of Logic, Methodology, and Philosophy of Science, Hannover*, New York, North-Holland Publishing Co.: 299-313

McKay Th., Nelson M. (2010), "The De Re/De Dicto Distinction", supplement to "Propositional Attitude Reports", *Stanford Encyclopedia of Philosophy*

Martin M.G.F. (2002), "The Transparency of Experience", *Mind & Language*, 4(4): 376-425

Meini C. (2001), *La psicologia ingenua: Una teoria evolutiva*, Milano, McGraw-Hill

Meini C., Voltolini A. (2010), "How pretence can really be metarepresentational",
    Mind & Society, 9(1): 31-58
Meskin A., Weinberg J.M. (2003), "Emotions, Fiction, and Cognitive Architec-
    ture", *The British Journal of Aesthetics*, 43(1): 18-34
Mitchell R.W. (ed.), (2002), *Pretense and imagination in animals and children*,
    Cambridge, Cambridge University Press
Morreall J. (1993), "Fear without Belief", *The Journal of Philosophy*, 90(7): 359-
    366
Mulligan K. (1999), "La varietà e l'unità dell'immaginazione", *Rivista di Estetica*,
    11(2): 53-67
Nichols S. (2004a), "Imagining and Believing: The Promise of a Single Code", *The
    Journal of Aesthetics and Art Criticism*, 62(2): 129-139
Nichols S. (2004b), review of G. Currie and I. Ravenscroft's *Recreative Minds*,
    Mind, 113: 329-334
Nichols S. (2006a), "Introduction", in Id. (ed.), *The Architecture of the Imagi-
    nation: New Essays on Pretence, Possibility, and Fiction*, Oxford, Clarendon
    Press: 1-16
Nichols S. (2006b), "Just the Imagination: Why Imagining Doesn't Behave Like
    Believing", *Mind & Language*, 21(4): 459-474
Nichols S., Stich S. (2000), "A Cognitive Theory of Pretense", *Cognition*, 74: 115-
    147
Nichols S., Stich S. (2003), *Mindreading: An Integrated Account of Pretense, Self-
    awareness and Understanding Other Minds*, Oxford, Oxford University Press
Nichols S., Stich S., Leslie A.M., Klein D. (1996), "Varieties of off-line simula-
    tion", in P. Carruthers and P. Smith, *Theories of theories of mind*, Cambridge,
    Cambridge University Press: 39-74
Olson D.R. (1993), "The Development of Representations: The Origins of Mental
    Life", *Canadian Psychology*, 34: 1-14
Perner J. (1991), *Understanding the Representational Mind*, Cambridge (MA),
    The MIT Press
Perner J., Baker S., Hutton D. (1994), "Prelief: The conceptual origins of belief and
    pretense", in C. Lewis and P. Mitchell (eds.), *Children's early understanding of
    mind: Origins and development*, Hillsdale (NJ), Lawrence Erlbaum Associates:
    261-286
Perry J. (1986), "Thought without Representation", *Proceedings of the Aristotelian
    Society, Supplementary Volume*, 60: 137-51; reprinted in Id., *The Problem of
    the Essential Indexical and Other Essays*, New York, Oxford University Press,
    1993: 205-219
Piaget J. (1962), *Play, dreams, and imitation in childhood*, translated by G. Gat-
    tegno and F.M. Hodgson, New York, Norton (original work published in 1945)
Prior A. (2003), *Papers on Time and Tense*, 2nd edition, ed. by P. Hasle, P. Ohrstrom,
    T. Braüner and J. Copeland, Oxford, Clarendon Press
Pylyshyn Z.W. (1978), "When is attribution of beliefs justified?", *Behavioral and
    Brain Sciences*, 4: 592-593
Quine W.V.O. (1956), "Quantifiers and Propositional Attitudes", *Journal of Philo-
    sophy*, 53; reprinted in Quine, *The Ways of Paradox and Other Essays*, 1st edi-

tion, 1966, revised and enlarged edition, Harvard University Press, Cambridge (MA) 1976: pp. 185-196

Quine W.V.O. (1961), *From a logical point of view*, Cambridge, Harvard University Press

Recanati F. (2000), *Oratio Obliqua, Oratio Recta. An Essay on Metarepresentation*, Cambridge (MA), The MIT Press

Recanati F. (2007), *Perspectival Thought. A Plea for (Moderate) Relativism*, Oxford, Oxford University Press

Schiffer S. (1981), "Truth and the Theory of Content", in H. Parret and J. Bouveresse (eds.), *Meaning and Understanding*, Berlin, de Gruyter

Schmid H.-J. (2007), "Entrenchment, Salience, and Basic Levels", in D. Geeraerts and H. Cuyckens (eds.), *The Oxford Handbook of Cognitive Linguistics*, Oxford, Oxford University Press

Schwitzgebel E. (2006), "Belief", *Stanford Encyclopedia of Philosophy*, http://plato.stanford.edu/entries/belief/

Searle J. (1975), "The logical status of fictional discourse", *New Literary History*, 6: 319-332

Searle J. (1983), *Intentionality*, Cambridge, Cambridge University Press

Searle J. (1991), "Reference and Intentionality", in E. Lepore and R. Van Gulick (eds.), *John Searle and His Critics*, Oxford, Blackwell: 227-241

Searle J. (1995), *The Construction of Social Reality*, New York, The Free Press

Shoemaker S. (1968), "Self-Reference and Self-Awareness", *Journal of Philosophy*, 65: 555-567; reprinted in Id., *Identity, Cause, and Mind*, Oxford, Clarendon Press, 2003: 6-18

Sperber D. (1997), "Intuitive and reflective beliefs", *Mind & Language*, 12(1): 67-83

Stich S., Nichols S. (1992), "Folk Psychology: Simulation or Tacit Theory", *Mind & Language*, 7(1): 35-71

Stich S., Nichols S. (1995), "Second Thoughts on Simulation", in M. Davies and T. Stone (eds.), *Mental Simulation*, Oxford, Blackwell, 1995b: 87-108

Suddendorf T. (1999), "The Rise of the Metamind", in M.C. Corballis and S.E.G. Lea (eds.), *The Descent of Mind. Psychological Perspectives on Hominid Evolution*, Oxford, Oxford University Press: 218-260

Suddendorf T., Whiten A. (2001), "Mental Evolution and Development: Evidence for Secondary Representation in Children, Great Apes, and Other Animals", *Psychological Bulletin*, 127: 629-650

Szabó Gendler T. (2003), "Pretense and belief", in M. Kieran and D. McIver Lopes (eds.), *Imagination, Philosophy, and the Arts*, New York, Routledge: 125-141

Szabó Gendler T. (2006), "Imaginative Contagion", *Metaphilosophy*, 37(2): 1-21

Szabó Gendler T. (2008), "Self-Deception as Pretense", *Philosophical Perspectives*, 21: 231-258

Szabó Gendler T., Kovakovich K. (2005), "Genuine Rational Fictional Emotions", in M.L. Kieran (ed.), *Contemporary Debates in Aesthetics and the Philosophy of Art*, Oxford, Blackwell

Tan E.S. (1996), *Emotion and the Structure of Narrative Film: Film as an Emotion Machine, Translated by Barbara Fasting*, Mahwah (NJ), Lawrence Erlbaum Associates

Tennie C., Call J., Tomasello M. (2006), "Push or Pull: Imitation vs. Emulation in Great Apes and Human Children", *Ethology*, 112: 1159-1169

Thomasson A.L. (2003), "Foundations for a Social Ontology", *ProtoSociology*, 18-19: 269-290

Tulving E. (1972), "Episodic and semantic memory", in E. Tulving and W. Donaldson (eds.), *Organization of memory*, New York, Academic Press: 381-403

Velleman D. (2000), *The Possibility of Practical Reason*, New York, Oxford University Press

Vendler Z. (1979), "Vicarious Experience", *Revue de Métaphysique et de Morale*, 84: 161-73

Walton K.L. (1978), "Fearing Fictions", *The Journal of Philosophy*, 75(1): 5-27

Walton K.L. (1990), *Mimesis as Make-Believe. On the Foundations of the Representational Arts*, Cambridge (MA)/ London, Harvard University Press

Walton K.L. (1997), "Spelunking, Simulation, and Slime", in M. Hjort and S. Laver (eds.), *Emotion and the Arts*, New York, Oxford University Press: 37-49

White A. (1990), *The Language of Imagination*, Oxford, Basil Blackwell

Williams B. (1973), "Imagination and the Self", in Id., *Problems of the Self*, Cambridge, Cambridge University Press: 26-45

Wimmer H., Perner J. (1983), "Beliefs about beliefs: representation and constraining function of wrong beliefs in young children's understanding of deception", *Cognition*, 13: 103-128

Wittgenstein L. (1958), *The Blue and Brown Books*, Oxford, Blackwell

Woolley J.D. (1995), "Young Children's Understanding of Fictional versus Epistemic Mental Representations: Imagination and Belief", *Child Development*, 66 (4): 1011-1021

Young A.W. (2000), "Wondrous Strange: The Neuropsychology of Abnormal Beliefs", *Mind & Language*, 15: 47-73

MIMESIS GROUP
www.mimesis-group.com

MIMESIS INTERNATIONAL
www.mimesisinternational.com
info@mimesisinternational.com

MIMESIS EDIZIONI
www.mimesisedizioni.it
mimesis@mimesisedizioni.it

ÉDITIONS MIMÉSIS
www.editionsmimesis.fr
info@editionsmimesis.fr

MIMESIS AFRICA
www.mimesisafrica.com
info@mimesisafrica.com

MIMESIS COMMUNICATION
www.mim-c.net

MIMESIS EU
www.mim-eu.com

printed by Digital Team
Fano (PU) in July 2014